To Say One Million Times, Wow!

Essays on Awe, Faith, and Family from America's Great Outdoors

(AND SOME HOTEL ROOMS)

SARAH M. WELLS

Praise for Sarah M. Wells

"Sarah Wells brings a unique perspective to the domestic essay. *American Honey* radiates an honesty, candor, and vulnerability I find not just compelling but refreshingly rare."

—Robert Atwan, series editor of The Best American Essays

"Sarah Wells writes with absolute beauty and unusual clarity about matters of faith, human yearning, and the complexity of marriage. *American Honey* is a rare memoir, filled with gentle humor, pain, intimacy, honesty, and the occasional bison. A lovely and loving book by a talented writer."

—Dinty W. Moore, author of *The Mindful Writer*

"In a world fissured by division—in faith, in families, in politics— Sarah Wells offers an alternative: *American Honey*, a debut memoir that invites us to gather around the pool table, sticks and drinks in hand, and have a real conversation about the wounds we carry, the desires we feed, the work we show up for, the temptations we resist, and mostly, the humans we love—day after lucky day."

—Jill Christman, author of *If This Were Fiction* and *Darkroom: A Family Exposure* and editor of *River Teeth: A Journal of Nonfiction Narrative*

"In *Between the Heron and the Moss*, Wells beautifully melds the secular and the nonsecular, the divine and the human, as she explores what tethers and frees the questing heart."

—Kathryn Winograd, author of
Flying Beneath the Dog Star: Poems from a Pandemic

"In *Acquiesce*, Sarah M. Wells writes with an intense clarity, poems so beautiful on the surface that the gravity of their depths takes your breath away. Wells excavates the burdens and blessings of a given life with lyric elegance, with frank candor, and with a wisdom rare in poetry today. This is an amazing debut."

—Eric Pankey, poet and professor emeritus of English and the Heritage Chair in Writing at George Mason University

Also by Sarah M. Wells

Creative Nonfiction

American Honey: A Field Guide to Resisting Temptation

Ordinary Time: Meditations from the In-Between

The Valley of Achor: An Essay

The Body Is Not a Coffin: An Essay on Miscarriage

Poetry

Between the Heron and the Moss

Pruning Burning Bushes

Acquiesce

Devotional

The Family Bible Devotional: Stories from the Bible to Help Kids & Parents Engage & Love Scripture

The Family Bible Devotional: Stories from the Gospels to Help Kids & Parents Love God & Love Others

Contents

Prologue

"I'm giving myself a trip out west as a family," I announced to my husband, Brandon, one night a few days after Thanksgiving. It would be part of our family Christmas gift, our family vacation, my fortieth birthday, something special. "I want to do this before the kids get too old and don't want to go anymore." I listed off all of the reasons this is how I wanted to spend a good chunk of the summer: "They're the perfect age! We haven't been anywhere except the beach with them. Also, we'll do it cheap. Rough it. We'll eat peanut butter sandwiches and cereal, we'll tent camp, we'll stretch every dime. It'll be an experience."

Brandon raised his eyebrows. "That sounds horrible."

I brushed that aside. "It'll be great!"

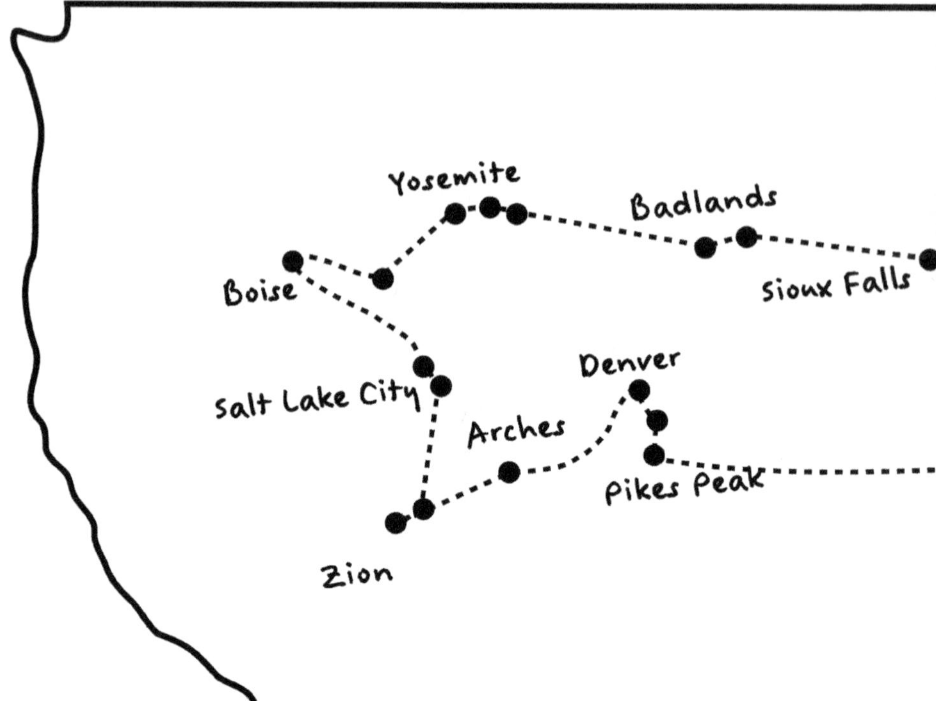

The Route (More or Less)

Home: Ashland, Ohio
Indiana Dunes National Park
Chicago, Illinois (The Bean)
Chain O' Lakes State Park
Sioux Falls, South Dakota
Badlands National Park
Wall, South Dakota
Mount Rushmore
Crazy Horse Memorial
Custer State Park
Cody, Wyoming
Yellowstone National Park
Craters of the Moon National
   Monument

Boise, Idaho
Salt Lake City, Utah
Antelope Island State Park
Zion National Park
Bryce Canyon National Park
Moab (looking toward Arches)
Pikes Peak / Manitou Springs
Denver, Colorado
Estes Park, Colorado
Kansas City, Missouri
St. Louis, Missouri
Columbus, Ohio
Home again: Ashland, Ohio

Ashland, OH
Kansas City
St. Louis
W.O.W.
Wells Out West Trip

Chapter 1

Knowing Your Limits

I woke up in the middle of the night in Shoshone National Forest on the eastern side of Yellowstone National Park to a bright light shining through the ceiling of our four-person tent. *Who is shining that flashlight?* I put on my glasses and unzipped the window a little. The river roared steadily fifteen feet away. Canyon walls tucked us in on all sides.

No one was shining a flashlight into our tent. It was the moon, making it look like dawn.

Ever since I first dreamed of taking this trip out west, I had envisioned a night like tonight, as far from civilization as we could get, removed from the harsh glow of city lights polluting the view of the rest of the universe *out there*. This would be the trip on which we saw the most stars we'd ever seen, I thought as we readied for our expedition into the wilderness. We'd see so many stars we'd be stunned speechless, so many stars that the sky would be all we talked about when we reminisced about our trip in the months and years to come, so many stars, so vast, so grand, and us so small.

But there were no more stars than what we'd be able to see from our own backyard in Ashland, Ohio, and certainly not enough to risk waking the boys at three a.m. My sons, Elvis (14) and Henry (11), were sound asleep. It would have to wait until another night, perhaps after we rolled into our second campsite on the west side of Yellowstone. I zipped the tent flap back in position and rewedged myself between my sleeping boys to try to go back to sleep. *What might be out there in the wilderness?* I wondered. *Could there be bears on the canyon ridge across the river right now? What if we saw a bear?* The idea thrilled me. Seeing a bear would be amazing and terrible. *Did our tablecloth smell enough like leftover peanut butter to attract a bear? Was that a bear just now?*

I fell asleep dreaming of bears, but by 5:25 I was awake again, the sun eager to rise over the mountains. I've been awake early enough only a half dozen times to see the sky turn from pitch black to its first hint of color, usually after waking at four a.m. to drive to some vacation destination. During those moments, the sunrise was a backdrop to whatever adventure awaited us. In the Shoshone National Forest wilderness, the sunrise is the show. Sit still and *watch.*

The sun began to light the sky three hours before its final bright debut over the mountains. But it isn't the sun that is rising, it's us. Our planet is taking the slow, long turn toward light; it's my continent that's taking another peek at day. The sun, that stalwart orb, is just out there perpetually glowing, spinning our whole solar system around in a galaxy that is speeding away, increasingly fleeing from its place of origin, ever leaving the Center and cleaving to whatever particles it can accumulate these billions of years.

Here I am, repeating the patterns of the entire universe in my very own minute collection of particles, leaving and cleaving, looking up, or out, as time accelerates with the more years I accumulate, all while the sun begins to obscure the galactic world beyond our atmosphere.

On the knife-edge of turning forty, in the same reorienting light of the rising Earth turning toward the Sun, the largeness of my own life is beginning to feel so much smaller, eclipsed by all that stretches beyond me—my growing children, my aging parents, my changing marriage, my evolving career—it turns out that none of it is the center of the universe. All of it, that is, all of my life, is moving swiftly toward the turn in the sonnet, the second half, the back nine.

As Shoshone National Forest made its slow, steady return into the sun's light, I practiced deep breathing, inhaling the canyon's aromatic blend of gardenia, sagebrush, and fir, and listened to the roar of the river next to our tent. I stood in the midst of it all. The river continued to roar. The canyon shrubs caught the breeze and danced. The Earth continued to tilt toward the light. It didn't matter if I walked or ran, sat down or slept, stuck around or left. The canyon didn't need me, but it made space for me. At that moment, in that space, I was sure: Only the most generous, creative, abundant, powerful, majestic, mysterious God could have conjured up such a place. No matter how quickly the rest of my life is spinning, I get to be here, now.

This is what I wanted on this trip I'd nicknamed WOW—Wells Out West—I wanted to experience awe. To bask in wonder. To say one million times, *WOW*. After having driven several days across the country, we had arrived in this one spot. Shoshone National Forest had delivered WOW and then some. The clear, cool North Fork of the Shoshone River surged with recent rainfall just feet away from our tent, tucked in a valley surrounded by mountains coated with Douglas fir and large juniper. It was hard to imagine a more perfect wilderness. I wanted to be moved by the majestic, and I wanted my children to have the same chance to be so moved. This is all I want from life at this point, to be struck in every cell by holiness until it seeps out of me in the form of joy and light. Is that really so much to ask?

Once the sun finally arrived in full and began its great advance across the sky, the boys and I ate a quick breakfast of granola bars and apples and then packed up. We jammed the tent and its poles into the vinyl bag and flung it on top of the rest of our stuff in the back of our blue F-150 adventure mobile, tugging down the truck bed cover and slamming the tailgate shut. In our final Shoshone act, we left the flat air mattress we used as an improvised tarp in the trash can and then pointed the truck toward Yellowstone.

The east entrance into Yellowstone was almost empty of other travelers as the three of us wheeled up and down and around the curving road deeper into the wilderness. It was as if the park was only ours. I rolled down the windows of our truck and gasped at the landscape, urging my boys every fifteen seconds to look up, look out, snap photos, and take in the view. After a thousand muttered "wows" with a few "This is awesome," "How amazing," and "Beautiful" tossed in for variation, after I made eye contact with a slow-moving bison, after watching the mud and guts of the earth bubble up to the surface and cause all kinds of stink, after we stood on the edge of mountains, seeing the tops of other mountains a hundred miles in the distance, after leaning over and feeling the spray of waterfalls, touching the snow that still coats pockets at the top of Mount Washburn even in the heat of July, after eating lunch next to trees with scratch marks made by elk, after all of this, we began our collective meltdown.

It started with my middle son, Elvis. We wrapped up meal #1,622 of peanut butter sandwiches, apples, and potato chips.

"Elvis, will you take these scraps to the trash?" I asked.

He groaned and pushed his mop of fuzzy, bleached blond hair out of his angry teenager eyes. "Henry, take this to the trash."

"No, you do it," Henry retorted, testing whether he could defy his role as his brother's indentured servant. Henry was on the edge of his own life transition, tipping toward puberty. Soon his voice would deepen to a baritone, his jawline would sharpen, and he'd stretch to a half foot taller than me. For now, he was still my big little boy, my sweet Henry with the easy grin, chubby cheeks, bright brown eyes, and ready hug.

Elvis didn't think Henry was all that sweet. Sulfuric clouds ascended out of Elvis's ears.

"Fine," Elvis said, whisking up the crumpled aluminum foil and apple cores and stomping off to the trash can. His wiry frame marched ahead of us, taking long strides in his cargo pants. When Elvis was younger and easily excitable, he would take off ahead of us with his siblings, sometimes engaging what we called his propeller arm—his left arm swinging in wide circles as he skipped or ran. That's how we knew Elvis was really excited about whatever was ahead of us. Where was that propeller arm now?

As Elvis stormed away, I rolled my eyes at Henry and gave him a quick grin of encouragement—*It's okay, buddy, I see you.*

I allowed Elvis to opt out of the next couple of sightseeing stops along the Grand Loop Road. He sat staring at his cell phone in the back seat of the truck, wearing some Where's Waldo-esque fashion glasses and a purple turtleneck, a bold choice if I ever saw one for the middle of July. Henry rode in the front seat with me. We got as far as the Petrified Tree before experiencing awe-and-wonder fatigue. Henry's stomach started to hurt. I had a blistering headache. I squinted my already-oversensitive blue eyes at the dashboard clock. It was two. Time for a change of plans.

"Why don't we call it a day, go get settled into our campsite, roast some marshmallows, and start over tomorrow?" I suggested. The two of them nodded blankly, apathetic toward the Plan. I took off the faded olive green baseball hat I'd been wearing every day in lieu of a shower to get a better grip on the pain above my eyebrow. I closed one eye and punched in the address of our next campground.

Distance to destination? Two and a half hours.

Before declaring to my husband, Brandon, that *I'm giving myself an out west trip*, I first pitched the idea around the kitchen island at my parents' house at Thanksgiving. It had been percolating in me far longer. I'd turn forty that summer. My daughter, Lydia, would be sixteen, the same age I was when my parents took us out west. I became a freelance writer after my life was turned upside down by long-COVID in 2020. With a year of health and recovery behind me, a flexible schedule, and children who were still willing to go on wild adventures with their mother, a trip out west now seemed like perfect timing.

"Dad has always wanted to take you kids back out west!" my mom said, wiping down the countertop with a dishrag. "We should all go together!"

I smiled while the interior picture of my nuclear family's out west trip morphed into a remake of *National Lampoon's Vacation*. "Sure!" I said. "That would be great!"

"I wonder if they're still giving dam tours," my dad quipped, taking a sip of his Miller Lite. "Or selling dam bait." He guffawed.

I rolled my eyes, again, for the hundredth time since my sixteenth birthday when we drove from Vegas to the Hoover Dam, my dad and brothers laughing their damn heads off about the damn dam until I shouted from the back of the rental minivan, "Can we please stop with the dam jokes?!"

I never miss my cue, though. Dad's eyes twinkle every time.

As I processed the plans and dreams I had for our route out west over the next eight months, my dad teetered between passionate enthusiasm about repeating the trip of 1998 exactly to "Forget it," tugging his ever-present John Deere or Harley-Davidson or R&R Excavating ball cap tighter over his head and abandoning the idea altogether. As much as my mom talked about my dad wanting to go on this trip, it became clear to me that it was a pipe dream. We would never actually re-create the famed Out West Trip of 1998. And besides, this was *my* trip. I wanted to go where I wanted to go. I wanted to see what I wanted to see. There was a whole world of national parks in the middle of the country I had never been to, and it was time to remedy that fact.

A few months before our trip, Brandon and I walked our two Westies around the neighborhood like we often do. I take Ruby, the purebred who is dumber and wants to die by car tire, and Brandon takes the other—Izzy, a Westie/Schnauzer mix whom we call "toasted marshmallow." She is smarter but is terrified of sewer drains, so not that much smarter. Our walks usually begin with quiet dialogue about what we did that day, what's for dinner, who needs a ride somewhere, and which child needs to unload the dishwasher when we get home, often interspersed by comments about how ridiculous our dogs are.

Somewhere between Williamsburg Court and Thomas Drive, the rhythm of our conversation shifts. Our pace changes. Something mystical happens. When you walk the same route day in and day out with the same person, space and time open. We'd been walking through the last two years together, every day, through COVID and recovery, through work and church, kids and careers. Between Williamsburg Court and Thomas Drive, we shift from taking steps to spelunking the depths.

There, between the two streets, months before our departure, I regularly brought up the expanding topographical map of my out west dream.

"I'm thinking three weeks. That'll be enough time to actually hike and stuff," I told my husband.

"Three weeks?" Brandon asked. "That's a long time."

"I'm serious," I said, turning my ever-hopeful eyes to look directly at him. "I'm doing this."

"Sure, it sounds great, but I can't take that much time off from work," he said. Brandon is the realist of this relationship. "Lydia has work too, and her golf season starts in August. She can't take three weeks off from golf. And what about bears in Yellowstone? You know there are bears in Yellowstone, right?"

I sighed and glared at him. He met me with his own shining brown eyes and a smile. This is how our marriage operates: I dream, and he provides all of the reasons why the dream won't work, and then I re-calculate. Together we eventually come up with a perfectly reasonable plan, one that takes into consideration all of the worst-case scenarios without losing the glimmer of hope and optimism I have that everything will always be amazing.

"How about the boys and I camp at a few parks, and then later, you and Lyd can fly out to meet us somewhere," I suggested.

Brandon yanked on Izzy's leash as she lunged at some squirrels. "We should find somewhere that has direct flights so we don't have to deal with changing planes."

Now we're getting somewhere, I thought as we made our way around Oak Hill Circle.

On yet another walk I told Brandon about my conversation with my editor at Root & Vine, one of my freelance clients. "I talked to Stacey about writing missives from each park on our trip. She loved the idea. I'm going to map out a plan and a proposal. I'll get paid to travel! And I'm teaching in Boise at a conference! So is it really even a vacation?!"

See? This is a perfectly reasonable trip!

Brandon stroked his salt-and-pepper goatee and nodded as we walked side by side.

I pulled up Google Maps and a list of national parks I wanted to visit and planned our route. Eighteen days total, leaving on July 12 and returning July 29, just in time for my fortieth birthday on July 30.

I shared the detailed route in Google Docs with my mom.

"Here's the route we're planning," I said. Over the next four months I would say variations of the same thing, over and over: "I'd love for you to join us for all, some, or none of it. With Dad or without Dad. With the RV or without the RV. Just come with us! We'll camp! We can take turns driving! You can fly out of Boise when the conference starts or stay through Salt Lake City. Just come with us. Please."

For the past decade, my mom has lived with one kidney and a stage 4 renal cell carcinoma diagnosis. After her initial diagnosis, I stopped pretending that we would do things together "someday." The day is now. There may be no others. Over the last ten years we've succeeded and failed at that mission, but overall, my relationship with my mom has been one of my highest priorities, one of my cherished connections. She has been the most consistent touchstone of strength and love in my life, and although I had worked through a long season of anticipatory grief, I was still keenly aware of her abbreviated timeline. Who knows how many good days we'd have left?

My dad lived as if she wasn't dying. He believed wholeheartedly that God would heal her and pretended like she wasn't terminally ill, which was frankly easy to do. With long, dark hair and a bright smile, my mom has always been a healthy, youthful, physically fit 5'2", the picture of health on the outside. She's also just *young*. The same year in which I would turn forty my mom would turn sixty. We had much to celebrate together.

"Well, I don't think it's going to work out," my mom told me on the phone one morning, one of countless mornings we talked. "Dad just can't leave work for that long."

A few days later Mom called and said, "You won't believe it! Dad says we're going to go now! This is going to be great!"

Astounded, I replied, "Really? What changed?"

"Well, Dad doesn't like the idea of you driving all the way out west by yourself."

"By myself?" I scoffed. "I'm a big girl now. I think I can handle it." *I'm going to be* forty, I thought, bristling. *I've been out of his house and on my own with my husband and children for nearly twenty years. He thinks I need his protection, and that's the reason he's going to come? To accompany me? To chaper-one? Forget it. Just stay home.*

I didn't have it in me to actually say those words, of course.

"Well," I managed to say, "I guess if that's what it takes to get Dad to come with us, great."

"Can you believe he doesn't think I can manage on my own?" I whined later to Brandon between Williamsburg Court and Thomas Drive. "Like I'm still a teenager or something. Just because *you* aren't going with me to protect me. From what? Bears? Camp volunteers?" I stomped around our neighborhood like the toddler my dad thought I was. But I couldn't shake the fury, the hurt, the shame of it. He *only* wanted to go because he didn't trust me. Not because he wanted to be with me.

Over the next months, my parents would waffle back and forth a half dozen times.

Yes, we're coming!

No, we're not going to be able to do it.

I told your dad that if he didn't want to go, I'd just take the RV without him!

Sigh, I guess I'm going to give up on this.

"That's it! We're going and that's final!" my mom texted me ten days before our trip.

I threw my hands in the air. "So I guess they're coming?" I asked, or complained, or stated, or wondered, or raged to Brandon. The trees along our walking route shuddered and swayed in the breeze. Brandon shrugged and laughed the way he often does at the soap opera drama I narrate for him when it comes to my family, whom I adore, who drives me nuts.

I suppose I could have said, *Forget it! Please don't come.* But I didn't want to let them down or make them feel unwanted. I hate disappointing people.

The thing is, I knew I could do this trip. The whole point was to prove to myself, if no one else, that I was well again after two years of long-COVID, to prove to myself, if no one else, that I was recovered, healthy, and able against the odds to experience and explore the wonder of a country I had hardly seen in the previous forty years. I wanted to give my children memories and stories they could carry with them for years, memories that would outlive me. I wanted to give them a whole pile of dam memories. I was turning forty, after all, the beginning of the downhill slope, the turn in the sonnet, the Richard Rohr second half of life. My life was spinning out swiftly. If not now, when?

By the time the boys and I reached Yellowstone, my parents were already on their way home in the RV, somewhere between the Badlands and the Gateway Arch. With Elvis irritable and on his computer in the back seat and Henry clutching his stomach while riding shotgun, I had plenty of time to dream about the campsite that waited for us outside the west entrance to Yellowstone. I imagined it would be just as pristine wilderness as Shoshone had been. Maybe there would be a waterfall. Maybe there would be a shower. Maybe tonight would be the night we'd see the ocean of stars I'd envisioned. Maybe, and I was counting on this one, there would be an electric outlet for the pancake griddle so we could take a break from peanut butter to make grilled cheese.

Mmm. Grilled cheese.

Sometime around three p.m. I started to fall asleep behind the wheel, which isn't really recommended any time but especially not in Yellowstone with its steep grades, sharp curves, and occasional drop-offs. I pulled into a sight we didn't bother to see and closed my eyes for fifteen minutes. There was, presumably, something spectacular beyond the parking lot—a geyser or a mountain or a waterfall. Probably something you couldn't see anywhere else in the world. I woke up from my catnap with the piercing headache persisting, right in the middle of my forehead. It was the same headache I'd experienced daily after having COVID, the same exhausted, relentless, medicine-resistant headache that made me quit my job a year and a half earlier. *Will this be the norm for the rest of our trip?* I worried to myself.

"How are we doing back there?" I said to the boys, looking with one eye closed at the rearview mirror and pushing a few stray hairs away from my face, back toward my long, drooping ponytail. Even my hair seemed to reflect how I felt. I tried to smile to reassure them that this was awesome and fun and exactly according to the Plan.

By then, Henry's stomach had started to feel better. He watched the juniper and pine fly by out the open window through the glasses that had earned him the nickname Henry Potter, his wavy brown hair blowing in the wind like a golden retriever. Elvis's mood had lifted, too. He held back his poof of blond hair with one hand to keep watching whatever was happening on his laptop. At least *they* seemed fine.

We drove and drove, looking at nothing, trees and hills and trees and mountains and cliffs and grass and hills and rivers and cliffs.

After a quick stop at a grocery store, we finally rolled into McCrea Bridge Campground.

The previous night at Clearwater Campground in Shoshone, we were one of three campers, one of which was Walt, the volunteer camp host. I had thought, *I could do this forever.* I could be Walt, learning the details and secrets of my valley, knowing the creatures who walk into my camp individually the way I know the difference in the deer that wander through our backyard. You could experience God out here, every single day. I could be this tiny little speck in the universe, tending my tiny, important corner, simply existing. Maybe I could convince Brandon to join me, when the kids are out of the house, if we had a nice enough camper—you know, the ones with the double slide-outs and big screen TVs and air-conditioning. I could spend each day of an artists-in-the-parks program wandering among the sage and cypress, picking up garbage, writing about the canyon and the roaring water and standing witness to the sunrise that begins at four in the morning and doesn't stop until it makes its steep descent across the other side of the valley. I would be there to watch it the whole day, uninterrupted. Who needs other people? It would be wondrous. It would be awesome. It would be *heaven*.

I forgot that not all campgrounds are Eden.

We pulled into McCrea Bridge, which is also nestled against a river . . . just not one rushing and swollen with boulders. Boats and Jet Skis lined up at the dock to unload riverside. The nearby road roared with the hum of constant rubber against asphalt. Our site was hemmed in on all sides by rent-a-campers, screaming children, motorcycles, and giant RVs (you know, the ones with double slide-outs and big screen TVs and air-conditioning). After I parked, I walked over to the camp host, a one-eyed campground pirate with a limp who guarded McCrea Bridge with his cane.

"I thought there was electricity on this campsite," I said. It wasn't a question. I wanted, no, I *needed* grilled cheese.

He laughed. "Electricity! Arrgh, there's no electricity in this campground."

But . . . the website! The website, I was certain, said our site had electricity. I sighed. "Okay, I thought it had electricity. I guess I was mistaken."

With my left eye shut to try to alleviate the pain, the boys and I put up the tent and started to make camp.

It's okay, I reassured myself. *I am a problem solver. I can make this work. We will have a marvelous time tonight, even if it kills me.*

Our F-150 came equipped with a power outlet AND a DC outlet, but for some reason, I couldn't get the griddle to work. I had tried at the previous campsite and became convinced it was a glitch with the truck. It didn't work again at McCrea Bridge. This time, Elvis figured out why.

"Mom, the griddle is higher wattage than the outlet," he called from the cab of the truck.

Not to worry! I remembered to buy firewood! We'd just cook our grilled cheese on the grate above a fire. It would be perfect.

Don't you worry, my friends. The Wells family would eat grilled cheese tonight.

Elvis helped me stack the wood in the requisite pyramid and stuff torn-up paper into the middle. He clicked the butane lighter. His mood had lifted in the shadow of his mother's escalating anxiety.

The paper wouldn't light.

"Throw the fire starter in, too," I suggested.

Nothing. I struck a match and held it against the paper. I struck another match. And another. And another. The paper smoldered, then died out. The fire starter brick just pinned the paper down. Nothing would catch. Our perfect pyramid of firewood remained uncharred. And the children in the rented camper across the way were screaming, and the mom kept screaming obscenities at them, and the children screamed back and then added on crying, and Henry said he'd like to take a nap in the tent, which sounded great but then there were gnats gathering at the top of the tent, and I was coated in layers of bug spray and sunscreen, and the *wood and the paper and the fire starter brick would not light on fire*. This was not how I imagined our last camping experience before Boise. Worse yet, I was certain, of all of the nights on our trip, this was the last chance to see the sky filled with stars.

But the forecast was partly cloudy, and trees surrounded our gnat-filled tent.

I sat down in my camp chair, the love seat that had traveled with Brandon and me through twenty years of baseball diamonds and diaper changes, backyard fireworks and concerts, rainy spring soccer games, damp weekend camping trips, and *plenty* of other successful fire rings. The bolts and metal frame were rusty now. They threatened to break underneath my weight. I stared at the cold logs and started to cry.

"I don't want to eat peanut butter and jelly for the eighth time!" I wailed.

Elvis sat down in the chair with me. He rested his hand on my shoulder, like a man, and said, "It'll be fine, Mom."

I texted my husband from our camp chair. "We are close to a road and there are people yelling in their camper by us and there's no electricity again and I can't get the fire started and I'm going to cry because I can't cook food again and there are bugs and I have a headache."

Three little dots appeared and then stopped and then disappeared as I hiccupped and slicked away the falling tears. I didn't wait. "I think I'm going to try to find a hotel," I typed frantically and hit send.

As much as I had wanted to "rough it" the first week of our trip, it was time to be honest. I was not up for roughing it. There was the picture of myself I had in my head, a picture of myself with my brown hair pulled back in a high ponytail, muscles tight underneath a tank top and athletic shorts, calves defined and tan above a pair of rugged hiking boots, not caring about how sweaty I was or how much dust had collected on my skin because I had experienced things. I had slept on the solid ground. I had witnessed the moving universe above me in the night. I had hiked miles and bore witness to an evolving world and never once worried about getting dizzy.

And then there was this middle-aged woman, this sunburnt, migraine-suffering, makeup-less, tired-eyed, amateur hiker whose arms are kind of flabby now. She couldn't even start a campfire.

One night. I made it one night tent camping with my boys out west. Was I really about to give in that easily?

I've spent most of my life trying to wrestle the universe into alignment with my wishes and my will, determined to make the Plan work out.

But what if, on the cusp of turning forty, in this turn-of-the-sonnet, back nine, second half of life, I just released the tight-fisted grip for a minute and lived a bit more openhanded? What if I quit fighting for my way, turned, and just rode the current, bears along the riverside and all? What might it be like to float along each moment filled with the revelation that it's all held, no matter whether the fire starts or the chair breaks or the bear visits your tent or you spend a couple extra hundred bucks for a good night's sleep and a chance to experience gratitude and joy again, the Earth making its turn back toward the sun again tomorrow?

I took a deep breath, opened my palms, and gave in.

The cell signal in McCrea was spotty, but somehow Google made it super easy for me to find last-minute bookings, because capitalism! Five minutes of scrolling through ads and websites later, my finger hovered over the Book Now button of a roadside cabin complex, each cabin complete with beds and air-conditioning and a mini-fridge and a shower and, crucially, electricity. I texted Brandon one last time (his safe reply, "I'm so sorry, do what you need to do" finally came through) before I entered my credit card information.

"Well, guys, start tearing down camp, we're getting out of here," I told Elvis and Henry. Ever conscious of other people's expectations (of me) and afraid to disappoint them by overhyping whatever was to come next, I added, "I booked a roadside cabin. We're staying there the next two nights, but don't get too excited—it's rustic. It isn't some luxury place or anything."

I couldn't imagine a night sleeping on the ground with a pounding headache in a place that wasn't as beautiful as the last place we camped. I couldn't imagine spending the next day, our last day in Yellowstone, cranky and sleep-deprived. I didn't have time for that. The sun was high in the sky and heading toward the final horizon, Earth spinning swiftly away. I couldn't imagine this being the memory we made together of day two in Yellowstone, a good day turned sour and left to calcify into bitterness, the bad memory we might bring up like an ugly bruise the next thirty years, until our kids tried their own out west trip with or without us.

But maybe most of all, I just couldn't imagine eating peanut butter and jelly for dinner one more time.

Has a camp ever folded as quickly as the one we set up in McCrea Bridge Campground? No, there has never been a camp teardown as fast as the McCrea Wells campsite teardown of July 2022.

A woman has to know her limits, and I found mine.

Midwest Reclaimed Wood

Western Ohio spills over into nothing new
except a state name and dilapidated
dreams, old grove forests timbered and fated
for reclaimed barnwood cabinet doors. The blue
summer ceiling stretches all the way to Wall
with only power lines, wind turbines, and Shell signs
to scratch against its hue. I keep between the lines
and point to rows of corn all knee-high tall
as if it's something new, something untouched,
but every landmark is tattooed and pockmarked
with barbed wire, railcars, and tractors parked
in the shadows of old silos, left to leak oil and rust.
If we return someday, there'll be nothing left to see
but Virginia creeper vines and vacant lines of oak trees.

Chapter 2

Indiana Dunes
and Chicago Gangsters

"Mom?" Henry called from his bedroom.

"Yeah?"

"I don't have any underwear," he replied. "Or shorts."

I joined Henry in his bedroom and helped him rifle through drawers of winter clothes. He had grown, again, my youngest who has always been in the 97th percentile for height and weight, teetering on the precipice of adolescence. Everything Henry had was packed already in the bowels of the truck.

"Let's check Elvis's dresser," I said. The boys are almost four years apart, but thanks to the wonders of genetics, Elvis is tall and thin and Henry is tall and thick; for the time being anyway, they wear the same size. Both extra underwear and extra shorts were buried in Elvis's drawers.

Elvis hardly moved when we came in but I chirped obnoxiously, "Good morning! Today's the day! Up and at 'em!" until his wild-haired and blurry-eyed body began to move out of bed. The promise of many hours of uninterrupted gaming from the back seat of the truck was far more enticing than three weeks of seeing America's best.

I thought that at least one of the boys would want to ride in the front, but when it was time to go, the two opted to ride together in the back.

21

"Well, I guess this is it!" I told Brandon, climbing into the driver's seat.

We said our goodbyes and I love yous and I backed out of the garage right at eight a.m.

"And we're on our way!" I texted to my mom.

"We're on the turnpike!" she texted back.

I'm always on the lookout for beautiful things. The world is filled with them, hiding in plain sight, pulsating with order, pattern, color, and texture. I look for beautiful things and beautiful people, who are making interesting decisions about how to dress themselves or style their hair or decorate their bodies with images and words to help the rest of us understand exactly who they think they are. I'm a seeker of beautiful moments, things I can treasure in my heart, like the mother of God, treasure I can find in a field and then, like Jesus's parable, sell everything I have in order to possess the field filled with all that beauty. I've been on the lookout for beautiful things for as long as I can remember.

Once you start looking for beauty in ordinary moments, it's difficult to turn off that impulse. Besides, who wouldn't want to be blown over by beauty all day long?

But this is western Ohio, eastern Indiana, turnpike travel. What is there to see except semitrucks and power lines?

I looked anyway. With both boys absorbed by their gaming laptops, there was plenty of time and space for me to watch for beauty in the passing landscape. I alternated between cruise control and brakes when drivers didn't obey the zipper rule at lane mergers. Elvis had assembled a playlist of old childhood favorites from road trips past, including They Might Be Giants and BNL kids' songs, but once he fell asleep, I switched to my own library of music, free to just be me in the driver's seat.

This would be our mode for the next three weeks.

The landscape out my window was tattooed with irrigation systems and solar panels, more trucks than personal vehicles, cell towers and electric lines, construction zones, fields and forests and roads lined with chicory—an intractable blend of wilderness and industry. It is a familiar landscape, which means it's easy to gloss over, dismiss all its sameness. I couldn't pull over to examine it up close. I had to settle for admiring the long parallel lines of corn whipping by like a never-ending flipbook.

Look, I kept saying to no one who was listening, *isn't it beautiful?*

Three and a half hours into our trip, I remembered what I left behind.

"Forgot Elvis's meds," I texted Brandon.

"Well shit," he replied.

In April 2021, Elvis and I traveled to Akron for an appointment with a psychiatrist. The decision to go came after a long stretch of troubling emotional roller coasters and plummeting grades, despite Elvis's keen memory and academic ability.

Elvis's ability to cope with everyday life stressors has never come easy. Elvis spent his first days out of the womb in the NICU as a full-term infant born with respiratory distress syndrome. His condition was precarious until he started to breathe on his own, and then they let us take him home. Just like that. He was almost dead, and then a couple of days later, they let us take him out of the hospital.

A couple of weeks later, Elvis started screaming every afternoon from three to seven p.m., sometimes later. The doctor said it was colic, a term that basically meant cranky infant syndrome—no known cure. I was unwilling to settle for shrugged shoulders and "He's just a fussy baby." Something was wrong with my kid. I did what any good millennial parent would do: I went to the internet for answers. There, several pages deep, another parent had a child who had been on antibiotics at birth and was also colicky. She put her Latin prefixes to use—if her baby had been on *anti*biotics, she probably needed *pro*biotics. Take away some -biotics, put in some new -biotics. Of course! This made a world of sense to me.

I found a local nutrition supplements store that carried infant probiotics and gave it a whirl.

We fed Elvis his mid-afternoon bottle and waited for him to turn fussy. And waited. And waited. He took a nap. We changed him. He woke up hungry. He ate (with probiotics). He *smiled*. At five in the afternoon.

It felt like a miracle. No more screaming for four hours every evening!

We kept Elvis on probiotics daily for well over a year, terrified to take him off and risk triggering again the digestive pain he must have been experiencing.

As he got older, we faced other behavioral challenges. During his toddler and early elementary years, "time to eat dinner" or "time to take a bath" could drop him to the floor, where he flailed like an upside-down turtle. It turned out that probiotics couldn't cure everything.

Anxiety plagued him. "Anything can happen," he worried, unable to sleep. "Anything." That included him dying, me dying, Dad dying, and plenty of other "anythings" he never spoke into being. He was right, of course. Anything *can* happen, good *and* bad, but who can sleep when there's a vast chasm of everything possible being imagined?

When Elvis started destroying things that mattered to him in fits of frustration, we made our first counseling appointment and got a toolbox of sensory tricks to try to break him out of whatever lizard-brain, fight-or-flight trigger he'd wandered into.

We went for counseling with him again in 2019, when Elvis was twelve and unloading a daily dump truck load of negative self-talk. The counselor asked about whether he had any untreated traumatic experiences in his past. We talked about the NICU, a near-drowning incident at the local pool, and the time he knocked out his front two teeth on his bike.

"Boy, buddy, you've been through a lot!" I said. Elvis just smiled and shrugged.

The counselor recommended trying EMDR, a way to kind of re-program the brain's processing of traumatic memories. We went twice, rewriting the fear and terror of nearly dying with a new story: "You were always safe. You were never alone."

Elvis spent those NICU days strapped to the many machines that kept him alive and monitored his blood pressure and oxygen levels, a nurse always nearby in case of an alarm. This was the story his brain needed to believe—*you were always safe; you were never alone*—in order to be able to release fear's reign. In this way, EMDR felt like another miracle, a therapy that pulled back the veil of anxiety that cloaked my son in a guarded vacancy. With the veil drawn away, I could *see* him and see the *real* him more often.

While the therapy seemed to have helped with the negative self-talk and constant fight-or-flight static, Elvis's grades had continued to drop. Then COVID happened, and all of the normal chaos of navigating puberty was disrupted by a global pandemic.

As someone who has always been on the bright side of every shadow, I've struggled to understand how Elvis could feel so bad about himself. All I wanted was for him to see the miracle he was to me. The emotional roller coaster Elvis had been riding all his life was more like an emotional conveyor belt that kept looping and resetting each night. For years Brandon and I have felt flummoxed by his tantrums and exasperated by his inability to articulate what goes on inside his head. We've felt helpless.

So after a crisis call from the middle school, we decided to see the psychiatrist.

"Has Elvis ever been tested for ADHD?" she asked. I shook my head. "Well, it could be the underlying cause of his depression. If we only treat the symptoms of depression and ADHD goes undetected, it isn't going to get you anywhere." We learned shortly thereafter that ADHD was, indeed, what Elvis had been battling against.

The ADHD medication cleared the chaos in Elvis's brain. After months and months of feeling like a failure, he could finally focus, turn in homework, and complete assignments. His confidence slowly returned as his grades began to reflect his abilities. Again, it felt like a miracle cure.

But even miracle cures can be undermined.

Two months before our trip out west, Elvis came home from a weekend church youth conference underfed, overcaffeinated, dehydrated, off his meds, and exhausted. I don't remember what he said or did, but I lost my patience with him. Maybe I said, "You need to get your act together!" or "You need to start to take care of yourself!" Whatever I said, I said it with several exclamation marks, and it sent my son into a spiral. We ended up in the emergency room, worried he might hurt himself.

It was Mother's Day, and I had caused my son to have a suicidal episode.

By the time the crisis counselor arrived at the hospital, Elvis was sound asleep in the hospital bed. I tallied up the circumstances that had led to this night. After waking Elvis and concluding he was safe from self-harm, the counselor sent us home.

Exhausted and traumatized by the reality that *my son was thinking about killing himself*, I waded through the next day's pile of remote work, then took Elvis to his play practice. He was rehearsing to be Oliver "Daddy" Warbucks in a production of *Annie Jr.* We pulled into the community center parking lot.

"Now that I'm better"—by which he meant medicated, well rested, hydrated, and fed—"do you think I can have a sleepover this Friday?"

Now that you're better?! I wanted to scream, or laugh maniacally, or sob. Instead I sighed. "How about you go to rehearsal, and we'll talk about it later."

For Elvis, it was as if the events of Mother's Day had been erased from his memory.

Not for me.

I have been careful with Elvis ever since, afraid to let my son alone for too long, afraid to ask if he is thinking about hurting himself, afraid to know what's really going on underneath that cool melancholy haze. When Elvis is sad or angry or depressed, my heart worries that he is *really* sad, *really* angry, or *really* depressed. My greatest fear is that he's going to spiral, and I won't be there to stop it. I'm afraid to ask about all of these things, but I'm even more afraid of not asking the hard questions and then never knowing the answers again.

In the mornings, when it's time to wake up for school, Brandon takes each step into the basement where Elvis's bedroom is and prays with every breath that Elvis will wake up.

It doesn't matter that this happened months ago. It doesn't matter that he's seemed emotionally stable. It happened once. And once is enough.

Brandon and I discussed what we should do about Elvis's medication via text message as I drove. We ultimately decided to wait until Brandon arrived in Salt Lake City in two weeks. He'd bring Elvis's meds with him.

It'll be fine, I thought. *It's mostly to help him focus at school, anyway.*

We drove through Michigan City to Mount Baldy on the east end of Indiana Dunes National Park. I parked and let Mom know my itinerary for the rest of the day, even though she probably had it printed out: Indiana Dunes, then through Chicago to visit a friend, then to the campground.

"We won't be eating dinner with you," I reminded her so she wouldn't stress about feeding us when we got there.

"Elvis, Henry, we're here!" I chimed. The first stop on leg one of the Wells Out West Roughin' It Road Trip. I couldn't seem to stop singing my announcements. "We're here! Lunchtime!" I chirped, octaves above my normal range.

Elvis woke up, irritated that we all still existed. Besides not taking his medication, I guessed that he probably didn't sleep the night before our trip. I dropped the tailgate of the truck and rustled through the cooler and dried goods container to make our first lunch on the road.

"What are we eating?" Elvis asked.

"Peanut butter and jelly, of course," I replied, delighted. "Remember? We're *roughing it!*" This was the part of our trip that was supposed to be both hilarious and fun: eating cheap food, making our lunches together, sitting around a picnic table at the national park. It was all part of the Plan. As Mom, it is my job to manufacture moments that will turn into memories. I pulled up the camera app on my phone. *Smile! This one's for Facebook!*

Elvis groaned and took his sandwich.

"I *love* peanut butter and jelly sandwiches, Mom!" Henry chirped. "Thanks!"

The two boys are a combination of storm clouds and rainbows. Henry's rainbows only infuriate Elvis's storm clouds more. While Elvis's birth story was one of trauma and anxiety, Henry had only known love and intimacy. His C-section was unremarkable. We spent three full days bonding in the hospital. He never took a bottle. He is by far our happiest and most affectionate child, possessing emotional intelligence and empathy on par with Nelson Mandela. If Elvis would like to avoid us as much as humanly possible, Henry is here for every present moment.

We finished our lunch and dropped our trash, then took a picture in front of a pile of sand, purportedly the dune. Henry charged up the trail ahead of Elvis and me.

Mount Baldy is a "wandering sand dune" on the southern shore of Lake Michigan. Its 126 feet are currently unscalable, as are most of the dunes, in an effort to restore the natural habitat and preserve them. However, there is a beach access trail just south of the dune that cuts through some woods and lets out on the shore of Lake Michigan. All 126 feet of altitude change had us huffing and puffing like a bunch of out-of-shape amateurs. I practiced measured breathing and checked in with my body's autonomic nervous system—*Y'all good? You gonna make it?* They shook slightly but nodded, determined to be well.

I couldn't wait to see what was going to happen the rest of the trip.

There's nothing like the last few steps as you scale the crest of a hill to see what might be on the other side. As the sand gave way underneath our feet, the long horizon of Lake Michigan appeared.

"Wow," I said.

I'd been to the coast of Lake Michigan before, on a writers' retreat on a cold weekend in October 2015 right before my mom's stage 4 kidney cancer diagnosis, and in the midst of the dark night of our marriage. The lake had been a cool blue-gray reflecting a blue-gray sky, calm and calming. Today, the water was bright blue and churning, angry, more like the ocean than Ohio's much more mild Lake Erie, and stretching far over the horizon.

Later, when I asked him, Henry claimed this point of the day was when he experienced God's presence the most.

Elvis seemed indifferent.

We took in a few seconds of water and skyline and meandered our way back down the hill, into the truck.

I wasn't done with Lake Michigan. The Plan was to walk the Dunes Succession Trail and then swim in the lake. Driving from the east side of the park to the west took about a half hour. That same collision of industry and wilderness we experienced on the way to the lake was here, too, smokestacks, steel mills, and railroad tracks tangled with the preserved dunes, pockets of woods, and tenacious outcroppings of wildflowers, grasses, and vines, all reaching to take over what humans had planted.

It seems to me that two parties of humanity are in a constant battle for land—one to save it, the other to exploit it. I felt that tension, between extravagance and exploitation, between utility and beauty, as we waited at a crossing and watched a train of a dozen oil tank cars pass. Trains have their own beauty and romance to them, with their slow churn, solemn rumble, whistle, hiss, and chuff. My boys used to love trains when they were younger. They played with Thomas the Tank Engine and his friends for hours.

"Look at the train, you guys," I said.

The two of them glanced up at the passing railcars, nodded, "yeah," and then returned to gaming.

In a paper presented in New Delhi in 1968, a Senegalese forestry engineer, Baba Dioum, said, "In the end we will conserve only what we love, we will love only what we understand, and we will understand only what we are taught."

I want to tell my boys that they have a choice in this life—to love or to fear, to nurture or to destroy—but they are busy building and destroying imaginary worlds. *Look*, I keep saying, *understand, love, conserve. Isn't this place beautiful?*

The train passed, the gates lifted, and we kept going, through the industrial shoreline of barbed wire fences and vines, trees and power lines, all things made and being made battling for more territory.

We parked in the massive asphalt lot at the west end of the park. Elvis groaned and took his time exiting the car.

"That must be the trail," I said, pointing into the white hotness of sand and boardwalk paths leading up to and alongside a dune. "What do you think? Should we take it?"

"Mmm, I don't know, Mom," Henry said.

"It is kind of hot," I said, squinting toward the trailhead and shading my eyes with my hand. I chugged another swig of Liquid I.V., my lifeline to ward off dehydration. For some reason, I had imagined the Dunes Succession Trail would be forested, like a seaside jungle or something, not a roped path leading through the sand to pockets of scrappy shrublike brush. In the stark shimmer of heat rising off the pavement and radiating down from the sky, it didn't look very beautiful.

Probably wasn't much to see anyway.

Elvis looked at his phone.

"Can you please put that away?" I asked, irritated, trying not to be irritated. "This trip is about seeing things and being together, not just being along for the ride. You can be on your phone for hours in the back seat."

Elvis stuffed his phone in his pocket and marched ahead. I lugged the bag of beach towels and swimsuits and hurried after him, Henry on my heels.

As we walked across the parking lot and up the concrete path, I paused to take a couple pictures of wildflowers growing in the sand and others making their way through the cracks in the concrete. (*Resilience!* I thought to myself, like a 24" x 36" poster in a counselor's office.) We walked up the path to the shower house and concessions that marked the main entrance to the beach.

There, on the other side, was the lake, and a sign: *No Swimming*.

"Oh shoot," I said. "The water's closed."

The three of us stood on the beach and watched the waves roll in and out, the shush and crash hypnotic.

Indiana Dunes was supposed to take us the better part of the day. It was two p.m.

I smiled encouragingly at Elvis, who stood erect on the beach, annoyed to be getting sand between his toes.

"Isn't it beautiful?" I said. "It's like the ocean."

Elvis glared off into the distance. We stood together silently watching the water, void of swimmers. Henry danced ankle-deep in the waves along the shore.

"I thought you guys would be able to swim. I had planned to be here for the better part of the day," I conceded. "I didn't think the water would be closed."

Elvis stared at his phone.

"Elvis," I started.

"I'm taking pictures!" he barked back, jamming his phone into his pocket.

Wee! I thought to myself.

"Look over there," I said to him. "That's Chicago." He nodded.

Is this how the rest of this trip will be? Just me, pleading with my son to engage with this world? Is this how it will always be? Come alive! Why can't you experience the joy of living?

"Hey Elvis," I said, "If you could pick just one thing to do around Chicago, what would it be?"

His eyes lit up and he smiled that big, beautiful Elvis smile I love.

"Go to the Al Capone Museum!" he replied without missing a beat. I wasn't even sure there *was* such a thing as an Al Capone Museum. Of course, my history buff son didn't particularly care about Lake Michigan or any other natural landscape, but he absolutely knew we were near Chicago and absolutely wanted to see something about Al Capone.

I absolutely do not care about Al Capone.

When I was very young, our family went to Florida. My dad had tickets to the Daytona 500, and for some reason, we got to go along for the vacation. (Since I am my mother's daughter, I would guess she thought it would be *so fun* to get away to Florida, even if it meant "tagging along" with her husband and staying back at the cottage while he went to the racetrack. She probably imagined a tropical scene, with fresh citrus dangling from the trees around a sweet little cozy beach house that her own colicky, infant son would sleep soundly in and her kindergartener would frolic around in the warm sunshine. No matter what, she would be delighted to be somewhere green in the middle of a long winter.)

Every day of that trip, back and forth between the run-down cottage we stayed in and the speedway, we drove by this huge castle. Its marquee advertised a giant maze and a miniature golf course just beyond the moat. There might even have been a drawbridge. Spotlights swirled around the castle towers. I imagined that the maze was like something from *Alice in Wonderland*, with tall, green hedges. I guessed that it was the best place on earth, better, even, than Disney World. Every time we passed it, I begged my dad to stop.

He waved it off. "That's a waste of time," I imagine he said, or "That's a waste of money," or "Maybe another time," hoping my young mind would forget it.

For some reason, I didn't forget it. In my memory, we kept driving, day and night, back and forth one hundred times past that probably cheesy, probably cliché, probably overpriced castle, back and forth from the track to the cottage, where my mom watched cockroaches scurry across the kitchen counter, where my infant brother probably never stopped crying, where I wandered around in the sharp grass watching oranges fall from trees and rot.

With the shoreline of forty in sight, that's the trip memory that came back to me. I remember not going to a castle.

I turn it over and over in my palm, scrutinizing it from different angles, holding it up to the light to try to find the beauty. I am a maker, after all, and there's a New Creation to usher into existence.

"Uhh, I don't think we have time for a museum," I replied, laughing and scrolling through Google Maps to see if I could find Al Capone stuff. "But we could go to Al Capone's grave!" Nothing like beginning your trip into America's Great Outdoors by visiting a famous gangster's tombstone. "What else?"

"The Bean!" Elvis said. He was practically prancing and glowing now. *There he is,* I thought with relief. *There he is—my son.*

But I had no idea what he was talking about. I Googled "The Bean Chicago," which turned out to be a real thing also known as Cloud Gate, a shimmering, forty-two-foot-high stainless steel sculpture tucked in the heart of downtown Chicago. It was like my son had researched things to do along our route without telling me they existed, hoping that maybe I'd read his mind and suggest we visit this out-of-the-way tourist site.

Google Maps said we'd hit The Bean smack dab in the middle of rush hour.

Rush hour! *Ugh,* I thought. *So much traffic. Just to see a Bean.*

In my own reprocessed memory, Dad stopped at the castle, finally. He got me out of the car and we walked across the drawbridge, into the giant maze. He bought me a sword and one of those cool knight helmets with the red fringe on top. We went back to the cottage. It was sunny. I picked up oranges from the cottage yard and carried them to my mother. They were beautiful and ripe and juicy. None of them were rotten. She gave me a slice and smiled.

When the doctors took my barely breathing baby away from me and to the neonatal nursery, I chose to believe that no matter what happened, we would be okay. That was the mysterious, miraculous word from God I got that week: No matter what happened, he was always safe. He was never alone. And I believed it, even when it was unclear if he would ever leave the hospital. All would be well, no matter what happened. No matter what.

When Elvis doesn't answer in the early morning hours, I choose to believe he's probably fine, even though anything can happen. Anything *can* happen. He's just sleepy. He's normal teenager angry. He's normal teenager lonely.

Anything can happen. It will be okay.

A friend of ours calls this next season of life the "season of relentless loss." I can rationally grasp what that means. I can say with my head that all will be well, that anything can happen, that it will be okay.

But my heart is not ready for it.

We've called Elvis "Buddy" ever since he was a little guy, our little buddy. He was such a cute little peanut of a kid! It's easy to remember the tantrums and anxiety, but just like the utility lines that stretch along the roadways, a thousand sweet moments with our Little Buddy exist in photos and memories strung in between. These moments I treasure rise to the surface all over again when I see my teenaged son lift his head and grin, forehead smooth and eyebrows relaxed, eyes soft and warm, all signs my boy is genuinely happy.

And Henry hasn't always been Sweet Henry, either. One day, a video from when Henry was a toddler surfaced out of the archives of my phone. Henry had pizza smeared all over his face and was transporting some remaining bits across his plate using a yellow Matchbox dump truck. In the video, he's chanting, "Pizza truck! Pizza truck! Pizza truck!"

Off to the side, Elvis said, "Hey Henry, let me help you with that" in the sweetest, gentlest, kindest, tenderest older brother voice, no more than six or seven years old.

"NAAAAOOOO!" Henry screeched.

"Just give him what he wants!" I yelled back.

My Little Buddy conceded like we all did to Henry's demands. Elvis was wearing a blue Western button-down shirt and a brown cowboy hat in that video. For years, it was dress-up day every day in the Wells household. Elvis wore Superman suits and Mr. Incredible costumes, cowboy boots, and Darth Vader masks—sometimes all at once—on trips to the park and the grocery store. He preferred button-down shirts, fedoras, and ties as a kindergartner and continued to be the style king long into middle school. He brought his sense of fashion and his incredible imagination into every basement theater performance directed by my daughter. As a toddler he would fall asleep at naptime surrounded by a dozen books. He has assembled a million different Lego kits and knows the Star Wars universe inside and out, and if he isn't a senator or president one day, he will be teaching future senators and presidents in a university lecture hall about the history of the world.

But all I really want is to see my boy full of joy.

For all of the ways his physiology refuses to make it easy for him to connect with me, there are times when the walls fall, the veil lifts, the lights shine, his smile widens, and love leaks out, tender and true. This is what I want. More of that Elvis. More of *you*. So come on, Little Buddy, can I get a smile?

⊷⧉

I quickly tracked a multiple spot map for the rest of the day to time out our visit with my friend, Tania, and still be able to get to Mom and Dad's campsite before dark. We could do it.

As we left the dunes and the lake behind and drove toward the city, the landscape evolved, hedging out the natural to make more space for man-made wonders, man-made tombstones, man-made towers, man-made mazes. I pulled into the cemetery filled with Italian names we said in outrageously bad accents, took Elvis's picture with two thumbs up over Al Capone's grave (*Smile! For Facebook!*) and then navigated back to the highway, inching ever closer to the heart of Chicago. We found a parking garage and not once did I complain about the fee. We walked to Cloud Gate surrounded by skyscrapers, tourists, and concrete in the middle of Millennium Park and not once did I remark about how bad traffic would inevitably be when we finally left, or how it would probably take twice as long to get to Tania's as we had planned, or how we probably wouldn't arrive at my parents' campsite until after dark.

People were everywhere, walking with purpose and looking at their phones, wandering around and looking up, standing and waiting for the next moment to happen to them, and there we were among them.

And there was The Bean.

One day ten or so years ago, I was walking from my office to the library on campus. Classes were changing and students of every shape and size were everywhere, looking at their phones or talking to their friends. And then the very same students were there, walking and talking, glowing with the light of Christ, shining glory. It was striking. I had never seen how God's love shone so brightly from everyone. I learned later that Thomas Merton had experienced a similar revelation, and I felt humbled to have been given that vision. Occasionally that vision sweeps over me again as thousands of the face of God walk around me, living out their miraculous existence, ruptured and repaired, reflected in the Cloud Gate.

In *The Seeds of Contemplation*, Thomas Merton writes, "It is God's love that speaks to me in the birds and streams; but also behind the clamor of the city God speaks to me in His judgments, and all these things are seeds sent to me from His will."

I am drawn to the wild places. I want to glimpse God in birds and streams, experience his Spirit in mountain horizons and canyon shade. But when I am in the right state of mind, my observer state of mind, searching for beautiful things, I remember that the human brain is, so far, the most complex thing we have discovered in the universe. Made in the *imago Dei*, the brain is capable of creating many masterpieces, from distant irrigation systems to metal shaped as a gate to heavenly places, and I am invited into that creation process, am doing it right now, typing about a trip to visit a man-made thing that is glorious and good and a gateway to the heavens.

The brain is also a wondrous thing, fragile and resilient, able to hang onto the shag carpeting of your first bedroom and the musty odor of your first-grade classroom, able to defend and protect, able to do whatever it takes to guarantee your survival, even when its fear is irrational. The brain can let go of whole years of moments and hang onto the plainest thread, and for some reason, it's that thread that forms you.

I have no control over what my children keep. I only have control over what I invite them to remember. And I want to be a manufacturer of memorable, beautiful moments.

Later, at my parents' campsite, after I asked Elvis, "Where did you most experience God today?" he would say, "Seeing Chicago on the horizon across Lake Michigan."

As the three of us stared up into the shining center of The Bean, I took a picture of our reflections. I wanted to remember that moment, that polished shine, the way it distorted our image and understanding of who we are, how we are, and where we are in space and time. In that reflection, we saw ourselves small, smaller than we are, and also far smaller than we imagine ourselves to be.

"Wow," we said.

The Waterpark Capital of the World

Enter the Dells. You have to make it past
an upside-down White House and Roman Colosseum,
convince your kids that the river will be
a far better time than the go-kart tracks
and cotton candy stands we passed to reach
a city park for peanut butter sandwiches and pop.
Now, for real, enter the Dells. You can stop
anywhere—it's just you here—then stretch
your legs along a pine grove path to a cove
where everything isn't plastic, molded to be
what it is not. Here, water laps at sandstone
sandwiched half a billion years ago. We
stand on grains of sand and watch our reflections
widen and flatten on the water until we become one.

Chapter 3

Where the Road Takes Us

"Sare, let's go for a ride," my dad said. He ambled to their motorcycle at the campground in Wall, South Dakota, without looking back, as if there was no question whether I actually wanted to go for a ride.

I questioned whether I wanted to go for a ride, but the mosquitoes were torturing us, it was still at least ninety degrees, the sun was setting, and at this stage of my life, when my father asks me to do anything, my answer is going to be *yes*. So I followed after him, the way I've followed after him most of my life, watching his worn blue jeans and torn-sleeved T-shirt lead the way, as if he was never in a hurry, as if he knew exactly where he was going, as if he was confident we'd arrive wherever whenever and at just the right time.

It was the first thing Dad and I would do together in the three days we'd spent on the road.

After the boys and I left downtown Chicago, we headed to my parents' campsite. By the time we arrived, it was dark. I was exhausted by the traffic jam coming out of Chicago and felt the tension in my neck and shoulders from navigating unfamiliar roads at night. The happy GPS announcement, "You've arrived!" meant two things: we finally made it, and I didn't need to pitch a tent.

Sure, call me a sellout on our Roughin' It Road Trip plan. There were plenty of nights ahead of us to rough it. Might as well take advantage of luxury camping while we had the chance.

Mom and I made up the beds in the RV while the boys poked at the campfire and Dad watched. This locale was strictly a utilitarian stop—set up camp, sleep, eat, tear down camp, take off in the morning. Ya gotta sleep somewhere between Chicago and Sioux Falls! I crawled up into the lofted bed above the driver's seat in the air-conditioned camper and slept soundly, the hum of my white noise app buzzing pleasantly next to my head.

In the morning, I reviewed the itinerary for the day. The drive to Sioux Falls, South Dakota, would take about eight hours or so from our campground outside of Chicago. I had booked a primitive site in Big Sioux Recreation Area in Brandon, South Dakota. No electricity, no showers, just gravel and grass and trees, and peanut butter and jelly.

That was before I knew my parents would be following us in the RV.

Mom had reserved a place at Yogi Bear's Jellystone Park. Yogi Bear's Park had a jumping pillow and a pool. Yogi Bear's Park had free WiFi and high-speed internet. Yogi Bear's Park had a general store.

How committed was I to this idea of roughing it?

Not very committed at all.

The boys and I left around the same time as my parents, pointed in the same direction, down the same highway. Shortly before lunch, I texted my mom that I was going to take a detour to the Dells of the Wisconsin River, which, according to my Googling-while-driving, looked like a beautiful place to eat lunch and hike a little. Mom gave a thumbs-up, and after getting pops from a vending machine for fifty cents like we were outside Marc's in 1990, the boys and I found a trail down to a quiet spot where the rock cliffs dropped straight into the water. It was just the kind of grounding I needed to refuel for the next stretch of highway. The boys bounded off trees and rocks like a pair of amateur parkour gymnasts before standing with me near the quiet shore. Henry and I watched a family of ducks paddle along the edge while Elvis did whatever he does when he's looking at his phone. We soaked in the silence around us long enough for the mallard ducklings to make it across the lake, and then we set off for Sioux Falls.

Mom and Dad reached Yogi Bear's Jellystone Park before we did. Their indoor/outdoor rug was splayed in front of the picnic table, SiriusXM's Outlaw Country sang in twang from the Bluetooth speaker, and folding chairs were arranged around the firepit no one in their right minds wanted to ignite.

It was so hot.

With a long, boring drive behind us, I settled into one of my parents' chairs and took in our surroundings. Camping is so different today compared to when I was a kid. My parents' massive RV means every campground they book ideally needs to have pull-through sites. They've come a long way from the pop-up and pull-behinds of my youth, and so have the rest of the campers. Up and down the rows of Yogi Bear's Park were veritable traveling houses with sides that slide out to add more floor space inside. They had full kitchens and primary bedrooms. They had closet space and bathtubs. They had air-conditioning.

It used to be that when you camped, you spent time in the Great Outdoors, but now it seems like camping means rolling your home into the wilderness so you can continue spending time in the Great Indoors. Above the half-hearted, heat-soaked trill of occasional birdsong, air-conditioning units whirred around us. Through camper windows, flat-screen TVs flashed silently.

I sniffed judgmentally at all of our neighbors and bemoaned the state of things. "When I was a kid . . ." I said, out loud, to my own kids. Elvis stared at his phone and tapped his foot against the dirt around the empty fire ring. Henry had already gone and returned from the giant jumping pillow, complaining about being hot and going to the pool to cool off, only to return complaining about the chlorine, the temperature of the water (so warm!), the fact that Elvis wasn't willing to go with him, and that I wasn't either, and neither was my mom.

"Back in my day," I started. We didn't go *swimming* in a *pool* when we camped. We put our swimsuits on and pedaled our bikes all the way around Punderson Lake to reach the public swimming area and then waded into that silty brown water to frolic with glee with the minnows. We didn't have a giant jumping pillow or internet access or mini golf or laser tag; we rode our bikes down to the metal playground equipment and got slivers of mulch stuck in our shoes. We waited in line to climb that tall, stainless steel death slide that scalded your butt and the backs of your thighs as you "slid," or rather, bonded to the metal, inching your way down. And then we ran to the teeter-totters to give each other "cherry bombs," leaping off the seesaw to slam down the person up top until someone got the wind knocked out of them.

And we liked it!

But Elvis was tucked into a lawn chair playing a game on his phone, and Henry had decided to take a shower after swimming because, *ew, the chlorine, Mom,* and no one cared what it was like when I was a kid because they just know what it's like to be them right now.

And it's hot. And camping's boring.

Dad sat in his own folding chair with a beer cracked open, exhausted from the drive. Mom was inside the camper preparing dinner, which meant I didn't have to. I'd make a point of helping clean up after. I slouched and let my legs sprawl out, sinking deeper into the nylon sling of the camp chair, and sighed.

All of the things we used to do when we camped in my youth continued to loop through my mind: collecting sticks from the nearby woods to add to the firepit, the games of rummy and Yahtzee, the toasted marshmallows over the fire, the hobo pies that scalded the roof of your mouth with hot cherry pie filling when you failed to wait long enough for them to cool. Most of the time, my mom was the one with us at the campground; my dad usually worked all day Friday and sometimes part of the day Saturday, showing up at the campsite for dinner and time around the campfire.

Anytime I'm sitting by a campfire, I remember those rare nights my dad and mom and I would sit around the fire with my brothers, the wood crackling and lifting its ashes heavenward, my dad telling his favorite story about the guy with the wooden eye who was super self-conscious about his fake eye until finally, one day, he got up the nerve to ask out a girl with a big nose, and when she said, "Oh, would I?" he shouted and pointed, "Big nose! Big nose!"

We're miles and miles from that campfire now.

Sitting there with my dad and my boys while my mom was inside the camper, I didn't know what to say that would be safe. I can talk to my mom about anything and everything, but Dad? Most subjects feel off-limits. We had managed to navigate the political land mines of the last six years without too much collateral damage between us, just the occasional jab and taunt about presidential candidates. I had called to check in on him on January 6 to confirm he wasn't on his way to Washington, DC. We could be passionate and opinionated, but underneath our differences of opinion, we were still family, and that's what mattered most.

That all changed last summer, when my dad and I got into it about how Brandon and I were parenting our teens as they questioned their identities. My technophobic father had been sent a screenshot of my daughter's latest social media post, and now the news was out. We could disagree about politics, but apparently we couldn't disagree about sexuality.

"Tell her to like boys!" he shouted at me. We were standing in their living room, my precious children safely outside, out of earshot, swimming in my parents' pool.

"I don't think that's how it works," I said, trying to stay calm. Both Lydia and Elvis had talked to us in the last six months about their sexual identities. Lydia told me that she was bi in a hotel room on the way home from visiting the other set of grandparents in Florida. A month later, after dinner one evening, Elvis quietly shared with us that he was gay. We were grateful they knew us well enough to be able to share this part of their journey with us. But even though we were ready to accept this part of our teens' identities, members of our extended family, community, denomination, and world were not as ready to embrace sexual minorities. The tension we felt for our kids wasn't whether or not to love, accept, and walk with them through this season; it was *how* to walk with them in a world that probably would not be kind.

I knew, of all of their grandparents, my dad would not receive this news well. Brandon and I chose to process how to parent in this new phase of our family's life with just a close circle of safe people, rather than involve my parents. That was over now. Our nuclear family stood in solidarity. Now it was time to take the next hurdle.

I had been preparing for this conversation for a week, ever since Dad first called to confront me about what he had seen. I had told him to wait. This wasn't a topic I wanted to discuss over the phone.

"She isn't *doing* anything," I tried to explain, standing in my parents' living room. "She's just trying to figure herself out. She's still the same Lydia she's always been."

Dad didn't hear me through his rage. "They need tough love," he sputtered. "We raised you as a Christian!" I kept an eye on the sliding glass door, praying that Lydia, Elvis, and Henry would just stay in the pool forever, or at least until I had time to grab their towels and my keys to make our exit.

"Dad!" I replied. "I *am* a Christian!" It was my faith in the grace and extravagant love of Christ that compelled me to love, support, and affirm my children. But being a Christian meant something very different to my dad than it meant to me, and the way we were choosing to parent our children wasn't anything like the way he thought was right, certainly not the way he remembered raising us. It made him furious.

"I'm disappointed in you," he churned out, shaking with anger and grief.

I felt slapped. "I'm sorry that I've disappointed you," I said, swallowing my tears. There haven't been many times I've stood up to my dad or publicly disagreed with him, but I had made my choice, and my choice was to love my children just as they were. "But this is how it's going to be. You won't treat Lydia any differently than before. She is still your granddaughter. If that's a problem," I said, "we can leave. Do we need to leave?"

Until then, he was all fire, and then with a whoosh, the coals went out, soaked in a bucket of my resolve.

"No," my dad choked out, "you are always welcome here."

We hugged, and I thought, *hey, that wasn't so bad,* except for the soundtrack called "I'm Disappointed in You" that began to run on repeat in my brain. Except for the tears that wouldn't stop dumping out of my face. I watched my father as he pulled out of the driveway to go back to the shop, watched him when he pulled back in, watched and waited for him to say something or behave differently toward my sweet daughter, who remained oblivious to the explosive argument in the house. We ate burgers and hot dogs, watched a movie, swam some more, and then headed off to bed. Nothing changed—he was the same grandpa he'd always been.

But it was different between us moving forward, tender, distant, more careful. I had made my choice. He disagreed. In the weeks following our living room confrontation, I heard from my father far more often than I had in past years. Surprise phone calls from him began to happen in the middle of the day. They might start out cordial, but then they'd veer right into a guardrail, him yelling at me some more about our parenting choices before I'd say, "I'm not having this conversation," and then hang up. But even those eventually faded away, and we did what we'd always done: We pretended like nothing happened.

Except everything was different.

"Want to go down to Sioux Falls after dinner?" I asked my parents. A year had passed since our argument in their living room, and here we were, on my much anticipated and celebrated out west adventure together.

Mom said yes, of course, but Dad declined. He was tired from the drive.

"Are you sure you don't want to come?" I asked again as we headed to our truck, but he shrugged and said no.

It was only a fifteen-minute drive from Brandon, South Dakota, to Falls Park. The Big Sioux River courses through the center of Sioux Falls and tumbles over an assembly of pink and red Sioux Quartzite rock outcroppings. It is some of the oldest and hardest rock in the world. Elvis leapt like a mountain goat from rock to 1.6 billion-year-old rock, pausing from time to time to capture his own footage of the falls. Henry stayed closer, marveling at the water raging over the pink stones. I walked with my mom around the rocks and lamented Dad's absence, like I always have, because even when everything changes, some things remain the same. I always want my dad to stay longer, be more present, spend more time, make more memories, and show more of his love. I am still forever entangled in this deep need, no matter how many times I have tried to just rest in God's love, to let that be enough. I had worked hard to protect my children from my dad's opinions, to preserve their love for him and protect the space that was left for them to have a relationship with him. And yet he had not leaned in.

My mom and I have been close, like sisters, for decades now. We talk nearly every day on the phone, and the ongoing litany of Things My Dad Is Worried About but Unwilling to Solve often peppers our conversations. Like most families, it's complicated. There are a lot of unanswered questions these days: about retirement, about who will inherit the family business, about how my aunts and uncles will divide up the family farm, about how his daughter is parenting his grandchildren. None of these issues are easy, none of them are solved, and all of them keep my dad awake at night, stirring at two in the morning to walk around the silent yard, staring up at a dark sky, and praying, praying, praying to the Good Lord to take care of it all.

When we talk on the phone and my mom laments about the Things My Dad Is Worried About but Unwilling to Solve, I often feel helpless. I just want to fix it. I want to swoop in and solve all of the Things My Dad Is Worried About.

Since I live a distant seventy miles away from the intimate complexities of our family's life, I am sure I have all the answers. Divvy up the land already. Retire already. Surrender already. It's the same way I feel about my teenagers' lives right now. When it comes to parenting, of course I feel like I have all of the answers for how they ought to live their lives. I want to protect them from heartbreak. I'd like to tell them exactly how I think they ought to be and who they should want to become, because I feel like I can see it—I see them reaching and stretching toward the fullest versions of themselves. Can't I just tell them who they are going to be?

But the truth is I don't really know what my role is in this changing season. It was so much easier when all I had to do was obey my parents and believe they knew everything. It was so much easier when all I had to do was keep my kids from running into traffic. Now, the world is grayer. Brandon and I have chosen to parent with open palms, to hold our children loosely and trust to the best of our ability that God has them in his grip of loving-kindness and mercy. We believe that their journey is their journey, and that our most important posture is one that keeps our arms and doors open as they tread the unmarked paths of their own identities.

Mom and I wrapped up our lament and called the boys over to join us on the ridge of rock overlooking the falls. The four of us took our picture there by the water, Henry with an open-faced grin, Elvis wearing his fashion glasses and button-down shirt, my mom sandwiched between her two grandsons, and me, smiling on the edge, trying to make the most of every moment.

The next morning we took off again, this time making an unplanned pit stop at The World's Only Corn Palace, because when you drive through South Dakota, you have to see The World's Only Corn Palace. Plus, corn is our legacy. My dad's family has been growing sweet corn on the family farm for decades. I bought a "Got Shucked at the Corn Palace" sticker for Brandon's guitar case. Elvis picked out a deck of cards.

The boys and I reached the Badlands around lunchtime. We made several quick stops to sweat our way through trails of ancient sandstone and siltstone formations that felt like treading across the surface of Mars. It was hot, so hot not even I wanted to hike more than a few hundred feet from the truck's air-conditioning. I refilled my Liquid I.V. and kept an eye on the park map I'd grabbed to see if I could spy any of the trails or scenic overlooks I had looked up when researching the best spots in each park. We opted to drive through most of the Badlands Loop Road instead of suffering too long in the waves of heat. We pulled into a vacant lot and stood alone in a field of prairie dogs. I took a few inadequate photos that couldn't come close to capturing the vast rolling hills around us, sighed happily at all this *nature* and *experience*—surrounded by wild grasses, a bright blue sky, and wind—then asked the boys if they were ready to go. From there we headed to Wall Drug. My parents pulled up on their Harley just as we were parking.

"Hey!" I said, giving them each a hug. "We're just about to grab some ice cream. Want to join us?"

"We just got the camper all set," Dad said. "We're going to take the Harley for a spin."

"Are you going to ride through the Badlands Loop? We just got back. It was amazing. Otherworldly."

"Nah," Dad said. "I'm not paying to go through a national park."

"You guys have never driven through the Badlands?" I asked, incredulous. "Haven't you been here a few times?"

He shrugged. "We've been up to the gate."

If it isn't obvious to you yet, let me be a little more direct: My dad doesn't sightsee. He drives, either a truck or an RV or a tractor or a semi or an excavator or a motorcycle, and when he isn't driving, he watches other people drive, stock cars in NASCAR races, tractors in tractor pulls, boats in fishing shows, or herds of cattle in old westerns. I think my dad likes the *idea* of national parks more than the parks themselves.

Before I met Brandon, I don't think I'd ever traveled to a city as a vacation destination. When my family wanted to get away from it all, we got far, far away from it all, uprooting from the rural township where we lived to even more rural campgrounds and state parks. We took occasional trips to amusement parks, once to Nashville, once to Las Vegas, but these were artificial places, as otherworldly as the Badlands, but in the opposite direction—so many buildings, so much traffic, so many people. It was marvelous and overstimulating, delicious and exhausting. These destinations were almost always gateways to *somewhere else*, somewhere *out there*. If we stayed in a city, we stayed on its outskirts and only dabbled in area attractions. Our road trips as kids felt as if it was more about getting there than staying there.

That isn't how I'm wired. I want to step beyond the gift shop, to root my bare feet in the sand and rake my hands across cool granite and dig my toes into the soil of the land that stretches out beyond me. I want to *experience* something, something more than miles and miles of highway.

Several years ago, shortly after we found out about my mom's stage 4 kidney cancer, I took her and ten-year-old Lydia to Maine over Memorial Day weekend. The Plan, originally, was to go to Prague and explore eastern Europe, the land of our ancestors—a trip of a life-time!—but Dad vetoed that. The idea of us traveling overseas without him made him anxious. Instead, we picked somewhere on this conti-nent and settled on a place the three of us hadn't been yet, setting a long-term goal to see as many national parks as possible.

"We have to do these things now," I insisted, leaving out *before you can't do them anymore.*

We drove together, stopping first at Niagara Falls and then making our way up the Atlantic coast to Bar Harbor, where we planned to stay for three days. *Three days!* In the *same place!*

"We *never* stay in the same hotel room for more than one night!" my mom said. We unpacked our things and put them in the dress-ers and closet. Mom surreptitiously placed her cancer medication and blood pressure monitor on the dresser. "I don't know that Dad and I have ever unpacked our suitcases like this."

Vacationing with just my mom and my daughter was unlike any other trip my mom had been on. I scouted out the best ranked, must-see trails and vistas in Acadia National Park, and together we logged miles and miles of trails, immersing ourselves in the rocky, rugged upper New England landscape of cliffs and spruce, fir, hemlock, beech, and birch. We climbed farther and longer than we imagined could be possible and reached peaks with ocean views, cool Atlantic wind whipping our hair into our eyes. No one complained once. As we chose our next destination, our dining location, our evening activity, we sighed collectively and thought about how easy this was. We are the perfect traveling companions, amenable and pleasant and patient and nimble.

If it starts to drizzle, no problem! If it's a little cool, we'll buy sweatshirts that say "Bah Hahbah" on them! We'll eat lahbster! The highly ranked shoreline is another couple hours' drive off our original route? Who cares! You only live once! This could be the last time we're in Acadia! Let's go! Let's see it all!

My dad doesn't hike. Dad doesn't pay entry fees to national monuments. Dad doesn't meander or wonder what's around the next corner of a trail or deviate from the beaten path, except by car, perhaps, to follow a rural route or avoid an accident or traffic jam. Dad doesn't visit a place; he drives by it. There should be an award for the most national park parking lots he's visited.

"Dad," I said, "Mom bought a *national park pass* that gets you into all of the parks." (Don't let your frugal parents miss this. It's the Annual Senior Pass, and it covers the entry fees for every national park for just twenty dollars for anyone over the age of 62.) I glanced at my mom and then back at my dad. She rolled her eyes. He shrugged. "You should totally go on the bike and ride through. You'll love it. It's amazing. And it doesn't take very long to make the whole loop."

"Well, maybe we'll get on the bike and see where it takes us," he said.

I nodded aggressively. "Yes, you should. The boys and I are going to get some ice cream and look around Wall Drug. We'll see you at the campground when you get back."

Elvis, Henry, and I spent the rest of the afternoon sucking up water and Liquid I.V., eating ice cream, and ambling around Wall Drug in the air-conditioning. In the grand tradition of families wandering through gift shops, we fought about what was an acceptable souvenir—*No, I'm not buying you the European version of Risk. No, I'm not buying you fake guns that look real. What does Risk have to do with Wall Drug? No, I don't care that it has an orange tip that makes it obvious that it's not real. No, really, I'm not buying you Risk. Please put that back. Please put that back. Look at these postcards! How about a magnet? Or a mug? Let's get some stickers. We should get stickers from every park we visit! Wouldn't that be cool? Why are you so mopey? Maybe you need to eat something. Why didn't you finish your ice cream? Maybe you're dehydrated. Can you pick something out already? I'm ready to go back to the camper. Can't you find something cheap and kitschy to remember Wall by? Henry, grab a couple of those free Wall Drug bumper stickers. Honestly, if you ask me about Risk one more time . . . Where do you think you're going?!*

After dinner, my mom and I walked around the campground, which was an awful lot smaller than what I had imagined. More like a crispy, grassy parking lot. I caught her up on all of the "fun" the boys and I had in Wall Drug while we swatted at mosquitoes.

The mosquitoes were fierce. There must have been thousands of them, and they were attacking as if we were the first humans to visit Wall in centuries.

Mom and I walked quickly, slapping at our calves and forearms and necks.

"And then he just" *thwack* "stomped out of the gift shop," I told Mom. "I wasn't sure where he went," *thwack* "but then we found him" *thwack* "just sitting on a bench," *thwack* "staring at his phone."

I swatted a mosquito on my neck and came away with a smear of my own blood. It was an onslaught. An ambush.

"Let's go back to the camper," I said. Soon I'd be one giant, swollen, red mosquito bite. My heart started to race. This was, once again, not the camping experience I had envisioned. Who ordered mosquitoes?! Why was it so freaking hot?! Wasn't there supposed to be a pool at this campground?!

"Sare," Dad called as we got back to the RV. "Your taillight's out."

"Yeah, I know," I said, swatting another mosquito and heading toward the camper door, the last great barrier separating me from bug-free, climate-controlled relief. "I think one of the bulbs blew."

"I'm going to take the bike and see if there's an auto shop nearby," he said.

A few years back, we all went camping with my extended family at Geneva State Park, a quiet, wooded, spacious campground in Ohio on the coast of Lake Erie. After a typical, magical Friday night underneath a canopy of maples with my brother's family around the crackling campfire making sweet marshmallow desserts, we woke up ready for a full, lazy day of camping, just like the ones I remembered from my childhood. Maybe we would fish! My kids loved to fish. My grandpa took me fishing while we camped. Maybe my dad would take them fishing!

"Where's Dad?" I asked my mom after breakfast.

"He had to go back to the shop," she said, "to change the locks."

We were an hour and a half away from the shop.

"Change the locks?" Brandon asked.

"Change the locks," I said.

Dad was gone all day, missing our walk around the park and out to the water, missing lunch, missing our decision to go into town, and eventually finding us in the stifling heat of Geneva-on-the-Lake's arcade.

It's a code now, between Brandon and the kids and me, for any kind of activity we'd rather avoid, for any time we feel itchy for something to do, anything except sitting still for a minute and just *being*.

"I gotta change the locks!"

Dad started up the Harley and pulled away from the campground to find me a lightbulb.

This stuff used to make me so angry. No, disappointed. Shaking with fury and grief. *I am so disappointed in you!*

Our family's time with my dad was so brief and far between, to flee or disengage or fall asleep in the middle of all these moments—it used to drive me crazy. Just as I'd arrive with the kids at their house, he would dash down to the shop to work. I'd wonder, *Why didn't he ask to take the boys? They'd love to ride with Pop Pop in the dump truck or on the tractor.* I remembered the half dozen times I followed my father around job sites, climbing into his lap and watching the bucket of the excavator scoop and swing the whole earth into something new. Doesn't he know what he's missing? As Elvis and Henry built Legos and played chess in the living room, as Lydia painted and baked cookies with my mom in the kitchen, didn't he see how great they were? Doesn't he want more and more and more of their time? To know them better and better? To see them, actually *see* them, for the miraculous and wondrous humans they are, whether they're gay or straight or purple or pink, into golf or tractors or history or dolls or whatever? They're wondrous! Fearfully and wonderfully made!

Now, though, that longing I had for him to know my children the way I know them has been replaced by resignation. It isn't okay, but it is reality. I needed to forgive my dad for not being the dad I wanted so I could love him for the dad he's been.

Still, I wish he could just relax. I wish the anxiety and burdens he carries could be set down for a while. I wish he could ignore the locks that need to be changed and enjoy himself more, enjoy his family, enjoy his grandkids, enjoy his life. I wish it didn't all seem like such *work* all the time.

But that is almost all my dad has done for decades. He works. He has worked so hard to make a life he can be proud of, to make a way for me and all my airy dreams to come true, to build a business his sons can benefit from, to furnish and fuel a home his wife can make into a sanctuary, to carry on his own father's legacy of farming and faith. While he was driven to make that life a reality, we were so often left with an empty seat at the dinner table, waiting for a moment to be seen.

He has succeeded, but I don't know if he feels like it.

I'm afraid that my dad will never retire and I am simultaneously afraid that if he does retire, he won't know what to do with himself. What will he do if he isn't driving?

Motorcycles scare me. In any other motorized vehicle, there's steel and aluminum and bumpers and doors and airbags to protect you. On a Harley, all that separates me from every other vehicle and meeting Jesus is hot air.

My dad has ridden Harleys for as long as my husband has known him. In fact, the day Brandon met my father, he pulled up the driveway behind Brandon on the first hog he owned. Dad was forty-four years old, and I was almost twenty, one year away from leaving his house forever. The motorcycle was my dad's answer to his midlife crisis.

I already worried about my dad dying, but the motorcycle really took it up a notch. Ever since I was little, I watched my dad smoke and drink and I knew those things could kill you; school and public service announcements told me so. I broke his smokes and shook the cans of Miller Lite he sent me to fetch him, as if I could end his addiction with a little flat beer. When he started having panic attacks and worried they were heart attacks, I worried with him. When men his age actually had heart attacks and died from them, I thought for sure that every unexpected phone call might be the Worst News. To this day, when my phone rings unexpectedly and it's my mom or an aunt or one of my brothers, my first thought is, "Oh no, what happened to Dad?"

I wonder sometimes if Dad's Harley gave him a release from all that seemed to be spinning beyond his control in that season. Life had propelled him into fatherhood earlier than they'd planned and then into business ownership a couple years after I was born. He was trucking along, digging basements and laying foundations for his children when, suddenly, his own father got sick and left him. Then, before he knew what was happening, his daughter was graduating, going to college, traveling overseas, meeting and dating and then talking about marrying a man, so very ready to leave him. How did this happen so quickly?

Now, we're somewhere in South Dakota. My sons are watching their screens in the RV, avoiding the mosquitoes. My daughter is sixteen, home with my husband playing golf and lifeguarding, making her way in the world. I'm the age my mother was the summer I met my husband. It was just yesterday that I was the mopey teen in the back of a rental van, gallivanting across the west with my dad in the driver's seat. I've driven a thousand miles in the last three days but somehow it feels like I'm just a hop, skip, and a jump away from that father, that daughter, arguing about boys and clothes, borrowing cars, begging for permission to leave the country, walking down the aisle, spinning to and away from each other on the dance floor. We're a thousand miles from home but still right here, navigating unfamiliar waters, still father, still daughter, but now so much older, so much farther.

How did this happen so quickly?

In the morning, my dad will spend the last hours of our time together replacing a light bulb on our truck because for him, love is fixing things. He will pull away the bags I've packed and get in there with some magic widget to pop the taillight away from the frame and untangle the spent bulb, place the new one, and then ask me to press the brakes to test the light. In the morning, I will wait to learn whether he will continue deeper into the wilderness with us or decide to drive back home, back through acres and acres of corn and soybeans, take the long miles through all of that nothing. Now that he got me halfway across the country, on the cusp of reaching some of the most stunning scenic vistas, I will wonder, will he choose to go with me?

But before all that, as the landscape turns black, we will fly across pavement, past cars and trucks that must be going tortoise slow, weave and bob and butterfly over the flat South Dakota roads that aren't flat at all; they rise and fall in rolling waves we ride so fast there's no chance the mosquitoes can land. We will rumble over the highways with nothing between us but hot air and emerging stars. As the Harley vibrates all his anxieties loose, I will hide my face behind my dad, wrap both my fists in his T-shirt, and hang on for dear life.

Photographing the Wind

We made it through the winding pass to tumble
into open country—nothing to hold back hot wind
for hours. Through the window, I try to capture
rain in the distance, seek the highway between
our truck and the next set of mountains, a promise
of respite from all this emptiness and heat.
I want to photograph the wind across
the desert, find the God Particle in these
miles, but how do you photograph the wind
except by what it changes? Who among
us knew who we'd be when we reached the end
of this relentless climb? How fiercely we sung,
how heavily we leaned into the angry gusts
for somewhere beyond the gnarled trees and dust.

Chapter 4

Along for the Ride

I awoke early to the white noise hum of an air-conditioning unit. I'd slept in the full-size bed above the driver's seat of the RV the last three nights, curtained off from my boys in their respective beds, fifteen feet or so from the camper's primary bedroom at the back of the RV.

"Roughin' it" had been abandoned back in Chicago, but tonight, we'd pick it back up again. Today we'd head out of the high plains and into the mountains, first to Mount Rushmore, then across Wyoming to the east side of Yellowstone.

The night before, my parents and I talked about the route. They weren't sure yet, but perhaps they'd go to Mount Rushmore with us, or loop up to Sturgis, or head northwest into Montana, maybe. My dad seemed excited about the possibilities of where they could go next and simultaneously terrified that I was planning to tent camp in Yellowstone.

"Is it about the cost?" he wondered. "I'll give you money to stay at a motel."

"It's not about the money, Dad," I said with a laugh. "It's about the *experience*."

"Get bear spray," he finally said, resigned to the whims of his crazy daughter. "I mean it. Bear spray."

I rolled my eyes and insisted that I would be fine. I'll be *fine*. I'll be FINE. (And, yes, okay, I'll stop at a camp store for bear spray. Everyone insists I need bear spray. Apparently people are getting mauled by bears *all of the time* these days.)

Although my mom and dad were thinking about continuing west, it seemed like this would be the end of our time together. That was fine—I was eager to get Elvis to Mount Rushmore and its Grand View Terrace filled with flags. I hadn't mentioned them to him, but I knew this, if nothing else on this trip, would make him smile. During this particular season, flags were Elvis's jam—state flags, country flags, obsolete flags, past flags from ancient nations—name a country and Elvis could describe its flag. He's a self-taught vexillologist. Yes, there's a word for "one who studies flags." When mapping out our route, I had hoped that my parents would join us on this brief trip to the Black Hills and the bulging stone faces of past presidents—it was the most patriotic of our stops, and my dad loves America—before they bolted off to their own vacation destination. Those were the only real reasons I had put Mount Rushmore in the Plan.

I used to feel differently about Mount Rushmore. Twenty-two years ago, I read *The Agony and the Ecstasy* by Irving Stone and marveled at the description of a sculptor in contrast to a painter. "If a painter blundered, what did he do? He patched and repaired and covered over with another layer of paint. The sculptor on the contrary had to *see within the marble the form that it held*. He could not glue back broken parts." In the Black Hills, the sculptor of Mount Rushmore found four faces in the rock of ages and carved the image of men out of it. He saw within the stone the form that it held. How glorious! How godlike! What a wonder!

But since then, I've learned more about Mount Rushmore's story. The mountain face of faces was sacred to the Lakota Sioux, who called the granite formation *Tunkasila Sakpe Paha*, or Six Grandfathers Mountain. The Lakota medicine man Nicholas Black Elk gave the mountain its name after a vision of the six sacred directions—west, east, north, south, above, and below. For the Lakota, the mountain stood for kindness, love, longevity, and wisdom. It was a place of prayer and devotion. They lived harmoniously with that marvelous slab of granite towering over the surrounding hills for centuries, until us Europeans came along with our chisels and firearms and trails of tears. Six Grandfathers became four Founding Fathers. Our monument to our greatness was someone else's sanctuary, desecrated.

After Mount Rushmore, I had plans to see the other defaced and refaced mountain, where the bust of Crazy Horse was under construction. I wondered, "Is this a legitimate answer to broken treaties and Indian reservations?" *It's The World's Largest Mountain Carving!* declared the website. *It's The In-Progress Eighth Wonder of the World!*

But what the heck, we were only a few miles away. Might as well take a peek.

From there, we planned to go through Custer State Park to experience "Wildlife Loop Road," what the internet told me was a "hot spot" for bison, pronghorn, deer, elk, coyotes, burros, prairie dogs, eagles, hawks, and more (!). After Custer, it was onward west, through Black Hills National Forest on Highway 16 across the Thunder Basin National Grassland, then through Bighorn National Forest on Highway 14 (and 16, and 20) to Cody, and finally, arriving at Clearwater Campground just north of the North Fork of the Shoshone River in Shoshone National Forest.

That was the Plan for day four. Without stops, hikes, walks, or gift shops, the trip would take us nearly nine hours and almost five hundred miles.

Totally doable.

"We're going back," my mom said under her breath.

"What? Why?" I asked, not surprised.

Dad had already taken care of my taillight and was busy packing up the motorcycle and unhooking the RV's hoses and wires. It wasn't even eight a.m. but it was already sweltering. The boys were . . . somewhere, probably trying to fit in video game time in the air-conditioned camper before they spent the day in the air-conditioned truck playing video games. We were at a place we'd probably never see again. Why waste any time looking around?

"Dad says Bill needs him back at the shop," she said. "But I don't believe him," she added lowly, so he wouldn't overhear.

I gave my standard Dad-is-disappointing response, "Geez, that's frustrating," and punched the Plan's route into Google Maps.

"It's my vacation, too," she muttered, turning away. Her voice cracked. "I guess I'm just along for the ride."

The stories we tell shape and define all of human experience. There's just no avoiding it. To interpret or communicate anything that happens to us whatsoever, we have to tell it in story form. I am, right now, sharing with you my unique human experience by telling you a story about my parents and their four-day trip to the edge of some of the most amazing landscapes on Earth, only to turn back because of work. Supposedly. I'm using a language we both understand so that you might find something in my human experience that connects and resonates with yours, which may or may not lead us both into deeper truths about our collective existence.

Otherwise, you're just staring at some intricate black etchings on sheets of paper.

But some narratives need to end. Some stories from the past need to release their grip on the present so that we can have a more fruitful and life-giving future. The nostalgic, heroic story of taming the wild west comes at the expense of too many other competing narratives. The story of human experience is always more complex than that. Knowing and honoring all of these stories gives us the best foundation on which to build an even better story tomorrow.

In her book *Rising Strong*, Brené Brown uses the phrase "the story I'm telling myself" to help people communicate the inner narrative of their experience. The story I'm telling myself is usually one-sided, often biased, and sometimes a straight-up lie. There's a story we've been telling ourselves for a long time about America that isn't the whole story but just one chapter from one character's point of view. Maybe if we quiet down for a minute to listen, we'll learn more of the story.

Here is a story I've been telling myself for thirty years: I can't sing. I *love* to sing, but oh, Lord, I can't carry a tune to save my life. If you want a good laugh, just ask me to sing. We'll both have fun, laughing together at just how *bad* of a singer I am. I've been telling myself this story ever since one of my aunts heard me singing (loudly) to a song on the car radio. I was probably eleven or twelve. She said something like *We should just turn off the radio and listen to* you*!* except she said it sarcastically, and I took her words to heart. Even if she didn't mean it, I heard *You definitely shouldn't sing loud enough for other people to hear, because you're terrible, and no one wants to hear you sing ever again.*

Since then, I've been shy about singing, or self-mocking when I do. I have thought of that moment in the car with my aunt a hundred thousand times. Every road-trip sing-along is accompanied by that storyline, "No one wants to hear you sing," and so I try my best to stay underneath the radio. When Brandon and I have sung karaoke in the past, I've expected myself to sing flat, and so I do. I laugh at myself and say, "I'm so tone-deaf," but I'm not, not *really*. Sometimes when I sing by myself in the car or shower or house, or with everyone else in church, I think, *Wow, that doesn't sound too bad, maybe I* can *sing,* but then someone walks into the kitchen. Someone tunes in a little closer and I become aware of others listening. The notes dip flat or rise sharp, I forget the melody, and suddenly I'm Kimberly Wallace in *My Best Friend's Wedding*, singing every single note off-key.

It's the "others listening" part that makes the record skip.

But there was a time when I thought I could sing. I was in the middle school choir. I enjoyed memorizing the cheesy tunes about pizza and fast food, which are, apparently, the only things composers think middle schoolers care about. Even though I was *so* shy, I had a solo. I felt proud. And then shortly after, my aunt said fewer than a dozen words and rewrote my internal narrative.

Now, it's entirely possible my aunt never meant to plant this seed of doubt about my singing abilities into my life story, but isn't that the way with so many little phrases that people toss about casually, how they find cracks in concrete like dandelion seeds and wedge themselves in? That long taproot of a lie is impossible to dig out.

But honestly, I haven't even bothered to try. Until I started writing this little reflection, it hadn't occurred to me that my aunt probably meant nothing by her words. She was probably teasing me about singing loudly, not badly.

Four percent of the population suffers from a legitimate condition called "congenital amusia"—tone deafness—and I am not one of them. I can distinguish between musical notes. I can match my voice to music.

I just don't believe that I can.

Just along for the ride.

From my vantage point, my dad has always dictated what my parents do, where they go, if they're going to visit, how long they'll stay, and when they'll leave. Even though my mom and I often toss out the joke from *My Big Fat Greek Wedding*, "The man is the head, but the woman is the neck, and she can turn the head any way she wants," the man is still the head of the house. His "no" goes. As my mom put it so succinctly, she's been along for the ride her whole married life. This is the story she keeps telling herself.

It drives me crazy. It's a story I want my mom to rewrite. I don't want her to be just "along for the ride," I want her to seize the wheel. At times I'd like her to kick my dad out of the driver's seat of her life and pull away into her own future, or at least switch seats for a second and not feel bad about it. *You could write a better story*, I think to myself. *All you have to do is go.*

Two months ago, my mom found out her cancer was gone. Just like that, the doctor said he couldn't see any signs of it. The death sentence was removed. It was miraculous, the way the weight of waiting for the other shoe to drop lifted so suddenly. There would be no other shoe! Just live! Just go on! Then my mom's mom died after years of battling cancer, alcoholism, drug addiction, depression, selfishness, fury, and despair. My mom had been her primary care provider for years, a thankless job, done for a woman who never knew how to love people well.

I wondered what might happen next. The two coinciding events seemed like a formula for my mom's freedom. I wondered, after all these years of being "along for the ride," if she might actually leave.

"I give it six to twelve months," I told Brandon. "Now that she has her life back, she's going to want to live it."

In the weeks before we left on our trip, I had pitched another travel option to my mom: If my dad didn't want to go, she could ride with us through the middle of the country, into Yellowstone, and out to Boise. She could come along and then catch a one-way flight back. That could happen now, too, I thought. But I knew without asking that my mom wouldn't want my dad to drive the RV back to Ohio alone.

We packed up and prepared to take off for the next leg of the trip.

"We should take a picture before we go!" I said. "We haven't gotten a photo of all of us together yet."

We stood with the sun in our faces and squinted at my phone, everyone mostly smiling, including my mom, making the most of the moment. After, the boys and I piled in the truck and pulled away from the RV and trailer, leaving my mom with my dad to figure out where the road might take them.

As the boys and I drove west out of Wall, South Dakota, the mountains made their debut on the horizon. I decided the South Dakota landscape isn't so much flat as it is dimpled, with smooth mounds and cranky divots that look small but aren't. It is flat in a long-climb-in-one-direction kind of way.

It's similar, actually, to the way my thirties have felt—like a long, steady climb in one direction. The climb hasn't been hard and hasn't seemed to change all that much, but then you hit the crest and see how far you've come. Behind you, miles. Before you, miles. And in those miles, everything has changed.

When Eric Church's "Hell of a View" came on the radio, it immediately made my chest ache for Brandon, which, admittedly, was the first time I'd missed his presence with my whole body. There had been plenty of other experiences to capture my attention, and we'd kept up a frequent text thread since I pulled out of Ashland. But if he was in the truck with me right now, he'd be driving, thumping his palm against the steering wheel to the beat and singing with abandon. We'd be glancing at each other and smiling, joking together about the boys and their devices in the back seat. When Brandon is with me, every one of my muscles relaxes. My body is at home when I'm with him.

Instead, I sang each line of the chorus to "Hell of a View" to no one with fresh tears in my eyes.

Our marriage has been filled with lots of solo trips. Brandon traveled with ESPN essentially every weekend for seven years. I tried to get away with him at least once a season, but most of the time, I stayed home with the kids. When he wasn't traveling, I took trips with the kids by myself, traveled to writing conferences alone, settled into writers' retreats with friends from across the country, and slipped away with my mom for days at a time. Whether by choice or by design, we've developed a certain degree of trust and independence over the last twenty years together.

When he first started traveling, I made plans every weekend out of spite. *I'll show him what he's missing out on!* I hauled the kids to my grandparents' farm, took photos of them at his parents' house, and posted happy status updates to social media. I wanted to have a good time with my kids and make memories with them, but I also longed for him to be a part of those memories. Those moments with the kids made me ache with both joy and sadness—*This is so great! I wish you were here to see how great this is.*

But after a few years, I stopped feeling bad for him.

The last couple of years he spent traveling, I swore by the saying, "Distance makes the heart grow fonder," partly because it was true—

when he was gone, all I wanted was for him to come home—and also to justify the way we irritated each other when he *was* home. Apparently, I couldn't load the dishwasher correctly. He kept making soggy chicken in the Crock-Pot. Who tries to roast a chicken in a Crock-Pot?! It wasn't just the little things; he seemed short-tempered and angry, like any move the kids made might set him off. By the time Thursday came, I couldn't wait for him to leave. And when Saturday night hit, I couldn't wait for him to come home. I missed his laughter, his smile, his voice. I missed having someone with whom to volley inside jokes and commiserate about our children's idiosyncrasies. My life without my husband is so much more serious and quiet, which is nice for a day or two, until it isn't. Quiet transitions to empty quickly. It was a long season of swinging between being married for four days out of the week and living the single life the other three days, one that eventually became unsustainable. The last season he traveled, I didn't really want him around any of the time.

During that rough last year of Brandon's farewell tour, I lamented to my mother-in-law, Rhonda, about our relationship. I spent a lot of weekends at my parents' and Brandon's parents' homes throughout our children's childhoods, enjoying the extra help and adult conversation in the evenings after the kids went to bed. I stood on one side of the kitchen island and she stood on the other, baking something or making something or cleaning up after baking and making something. The kids were most likely watching a movie. She had probably just offered to make me a cup of tea. We both love tea.

On my long commute to and from my job in Cleveland to our home in Akron, I obsessed over what it would look like to just leave him. *What if I got an apartment in Cleveland? I wouldn't have this commute anymore. We're basically just co-parenting anyway. I make good money. I could afford it. He could have the kids on the weekdays and I could take them every weekend. We could make it work. Wouldn't it be better that way instead of feeling like I'm walking on eggshells all of the time, waiting for him to ignite and explode?*

I didn't say any of that to my mother-in-law. Instead I said, "I don't know how much longer I can do this."

Rhonda's eyes teared up. Stirring a generous dollop of honey into my cup of tea, she said, "I know it's hard. But don't you want to write a better story?"

We both love tea, and we both love Brandon.

That was seven years ago. Most of the cells in my body have sloughed off and regenerated during that period of time. I'm basically an entirely new person.

And Brandon and me? We're writing a better story.

Back in 2005, the presidents on Mount Rushmore got their first facial. It'd been over sixty years—high time someone paid attention to their complexion. Workers had noticed that lichens were gnawing away at the presidents' faces, which would eventually leave them pockmarked. Without a thorough scrubbing, the granite would, over time, succumb to the wear and tear and drop a nose or eyebrow or tuft of hair. So workers took some scrub brushes and power washers up the presidents' neckline and went to work.

Take that, lichens!

Left untouched, scientists estimate that lichens would completely erode away the noses of George Washington and his compatriots in, oh, say, 2.4 million years. Their basic shape would be erased in around 7 million years. Humans will have left their mark on the landscape *that long*.

For those keeping score, our species, the Homo sapiens, has only really been around for two hundred thousand years, about 3 percent of the projected lifespan of our granite handiwork. But lichens have been in the business of erasing rock formations for far longer—hundreds of millions of years—and they will likely be around long after any trace of the presidents and the progeny of their sculptors.

Now who is the superior species?

Lichens aren't actually one thing but a symbiosis of algae, fungi, and yeast working in tandem to start the soil production process in lifeless environments. No one individual can take on granite, but a community? A whole community of algae and fungi and yeast can dissolve a mountain. Sorry, Paul Simon, no man is a rock, no man is an island. Lichens are the primary excavators that come in and transform an ecosystem into a habitable space. They literally eat stone and turn it into soil. Lichens rewrite geological history.

I've been wanting my mom to live a different story, but now that I'm really thinking about it, I don't think it's a better one. I don't even think it's an easier one. For years I have responded to my mom's complaints about my dad or my grandma with, "Geez, that's frustrating," followed by a litany of reasons she should "just" make my grandma move into a nursing home or "just" stop driving or "just" sell her house and move closer or "just" stop talking to her, cut her off—she's cruel and abusive and is taking advantage of you—or even "just" leave, if you have to leave, "just" do it.

My dad had missed so much of my childhood because of work, but my mom? She was always there. She was so always and ever there that it didn't occur to me that there could be a time when she was *not*. That's what made her cancer diagnosis so jarring. You mean this ever-present bedrock of love and mercy I've taken for granted my entire life could disappear? Not someday. Soon?

I love my mom with a fierce favoritism. I want her to be happy. I want her to be loved well. It's unfair that she wasn't often loved well by her mom and that sometimes she isn't loved well by my dad and at times, if I'm being really honest, she hasn't always been loved well by me. The justice-loving, earn-it-to-deserve-it part of me believes my dad doesn't deserve her love.

What kind of love believes that?

Just leave. You could just leave.

But she's never left. She loves her people with an everlasting love. For better or for worse, she doesn't leave.

In the rearview mirror of the last decade, I'm ashamed by the number of times I've thought about exit ramps. I wanted Brandon to just leave when we lived in Ashland, when his foray into stay-at-home parenting sent him into a season of depression. That was mile marker 5. At mile markers 9 and 10, someone else tried to get me to exit the highway of marital bliss, but several supernatural guardrails saved me from that potentially life-altering disaster. At mile marker 13, I wanted Brandon to just leave his six-year-long career of working behind the scenes in professional sports broadcasting. That was the "write a better story" year, the year I still loved my husband but didn't really like him all that much.

South Dakota rolls on and on, mile marker by mile marker, until suddenly, there are the Black Hills with their steep cliffs and tall pines and stone monuments to past victories and losses. We will celebrate nineteen years of marriage this fall. I talk about the off-ramps and detours as if they happened to someone else because they *did*.

We were someone else. Our marriage today grew out of the loam of those years. I'm ashamed by all of those possible exit ramps because here I am, now, missing my husband who I've been with nearly every day since the pandemic began in March 2020. I don't have any use for that saying about distance and fondness anymore. All of that togetherness made me fonder than ever of my husband. It turns out I really like being with my husband. Here I am, missing the husband I wanted to just leave, and secretly wishing my mother would just leave my father, secretly wishing my mother would have just left her mother, secretly thinking just leaving is easier than just staying, loving with some kind of steadfast love instead of this flighty imposter that isn't really love at all, just self-centered ease. Like love has ever been easy.

Love, true love (or "twoo love," as the priest says in *The Princess Bride*), *gospel* love puts so much more weight on the long view of things ("will follow you, *fowever*"). It acknowledges the complex, confusing, sometimes aggravating pockmarks and divots in the landscape while keeping its eyes on the horizon, recognizing that everything you're going through right now, together with this complex, confusing, and sometimes aggravating person, is shaping you into the person you will be someday, and you are shaping them. There is no shaping and forming without some algae or yeast or fungus. We're inextricably bound to one another.

Wouldn't it be really great if you stayed? If you arrived, together? Wouldn't it be so lovely to keep loving the person you said you'd love, even though they're probably depressed, even though they're definitely anxious, even though they desperately need some life raft that probably you could throw at them if you'd just see them instead of just wanting to leave them?

My parents married at nineteen and twenty-three, something like four or six or eight weeks pregnant with me. They grew up across the street from each other and played backyard softball together, one set of siblings against the other. When she was in elementary school, my mom gave my dad a wallet she probably took from her older brother. They've known each other their entire lives. Like me, my mom left her parents' house to join her husband's home. They started a business together two years into their marriage and have kept it going, growing and providing a foundation of security out of clean laundry, plenty of food, and encouragement to do whatever I dreamed. They raised me and my two brothers. They have fought and cried and disagreed and survived back surgeries, C-sections, seasonal depression, loneliness, and cancer. And they have laughed together, toured the country together, listened to live music together, rode Harleys together, shared jokes and intimate conversations and prayers together. They have been married twice as long as me.

When I started my own family, I knew I could figure out what to do because I was armed with *What to Expect When You're Expecting*, Google, and my mom's example. My mom told me that when she became a mom, she had no idea what she was doing. She figured that as long as she did the exact opposite of what her mom did, she'd be just fine. I have thought about this reality often. My mom is a cycle breaker. Once imprisoned in a home of addiction and alcoholism, she emerged wide-eyed and guided primarily by what not to do. And she did it; she changed the trajectory of life for future generations. For nearly forty years, my mother has shown me what it looks like to be faithful, what it looks like to love unconditionally, and what it looks like to stick with another human, even when it seems irrational to do so. She has shown me what it looks like to cling to granite, steadily changing the landscape until it is all made new.

My mom knows how to write a better love story than me.

The landscape from Wall to the Black Hills changed in a hurry. Suddenly pine trees and big hills were everywhere. After no green across the drought-stricken high plains, so much green! I rolled down the windows and turned up the radio, singing along at the top of my lungs to "Hell of a View." I thought about the miles and miles of open land, miles and miles of fields and forests, miles and miles of road signs and exit ramps, and I thought about the miles and miles yet to go. So many miles filled with redemption and restoration, trees growing out of ashes, lichens eating away at granite.

It didn't take long to get to Mount Rushmore, sneak a peek at the mountain, take a couple snapshots on the Grand View Terrace to prove we were there, and drive on to the Crazy Horse Memorial to see another mountain in the process of being chiseled away. It still seemed so arrogant of humanity to carve faces—any faces of anyone—onto a cliffside that was formed 1.6 billion years ago.

One point six *billion* years ago? The granite Mount Rushmore is carved from was formed 1.6 billion years ago—that's 1,600 million years ago. If Mount Rushmore's faces last 7 million years, our imprint on that part of the planet will have lasted .43 percent of the rock's existence. For perspective, if I live to the ripe old age of 100, .43 percent of my life is 157 days, or just over five months.

Five months is not nothing; after all, in the last five months, my mom's cancer disappeared and her mother died. My son thought about hurting himself. My daughter started driving. It has been a momentous five months of mountains and valleys.

But five months is also nothing. That's, like, 6 percent of a seven-year cell regeneration cycle. It takes no time at all to weave away from the carved granite cliffs in my rearview mirror, eclipsed by fresh pines and new mountain roads, no time at all to turn the page and ride along into another chapter of some far grander story.

Glory

Shoshone National Forest, Clearwater Campground

The rain just ended
    but the Shoshone River rushes eternal.

There is nothing human, save for
    bear boxes, firepits, gravel paths

to tent sites marked by wooden spikes,
    and us. We are just visitors, here for only

a breath of juniper- and sage-infused
    atmosphere, incense of canyons carved

by living water for the pleasure of creation
    long before some human stood among

the brush and exhaled. Now we stand
    as witness as all the wild world continues

its magnificent existence, me among it
    for a drumbeat, a whisper in some gradual

unfolding. Don't hold your breath. It will
    be hours of rising light in this valley before

it is finally day, but wait anyway—
    the whitebark pine, Douglas fir, cascading

river all bear the names we gave them
    and sing in this kingdom of humus,

mycelium, and stone—this slow, sudden
    unveiling, isn't it glorious?

Chapter 5

The Bears Out There

The first time I woke up in Shoshone National Forest, it was because I'd dreamt a bear had entered our tent. In my dream, the tent was the size of a conference center. It was my fault that the bear had gotten in because I had left a giant pile of bacon sizzling on a griddle to go find paper towels. When I came back, the bear was double-fisting bacon into his open, jagged jaws. I ran to find my bear spray, or Walt, the Clearwater Campground camp host. When I returned to the site of the bacon-fisted bear, a student at the conference was giving directions to him, only the bear was thinly disguised as a person. He had a plastic person face mask on, like the masks we used to have as kids for Halloween, with two eyeholes and a rubber band to hold the mask in place. And he was wearing jeans. Wait, maybe it was Smokey the Bear? The student was doing their best to calmly usher the grizzly back outside. How did he not know it was a bear?! There was fur bursting out from underneath his plastic-person face mask!

It wasn't the first time my former work-life has crept into my dreams, but it was the first time a grizzly had shown up. And bacon. I don't think I've ever dreamed about bacon.

When we first arrived at our tent site in Clearwater Campground, it had just stopped raining. Walt came over to give us the scoop on local bear activity before we set up our tent.

"Haven't had bears inside the campground in at least two years, and we want to keep it that way," he said. "Any bears we do get will walk up the river. Keep your food and drinks and cosmetics and everything else that smells besides your bodies in the bear locker or your truck, so we keep the bears out of this campground. The only real visitors we get here to this campsite are deer or sometimes bison, but keep an eye on the cliffs across the way, sometimes you'll see black bear or bighorn sheep and mountain goats over there."

Walt hovered and chatted for a long time, giving us a bear spray tutorial while the boys and I stood listening in the drizzle, holding the tent that he kept telling us we'd better start putting up before it started to rain again. We set up camp, ate, and engaged in a round of collaborative storytelling that quickly spiraled out of hand (you try this with two adolescent boys who contribute farting and death and see how far you get). The boys and I crawled into the tent just as the clouds burst open, adding staccato droplets to the churning symphony of the Shoshone River, the backdrop to my dream about grizzlies and conferences.

I've been dreaming about my work at Spire, the marketing agency I left to recover from long-COVID, ever since I started there in 2017. Before I resigned, I often spent my work dreams in strategy sessions, solving a high-level marketing problem or staring at a spreadsheet and trying to calculate someone's ROI. I would wake up with no idea what the marketing problem was and, worse, no solutions. Then, I had to go to work and live out my dream, except in real life, I found the solutions. (I was pretty good at my job.)

Post-resignation, though, my dreams of Spire have been first-day-of-work dreams. The whole team is so happy to see me again, but everything is different, and no one seems to realize I don't know what I'm doing. I spend most of the dream waiting for orientation to start, wandering from long corridor to long corridor of high-tech, Google-looking workstations where people sit waiting for the Monday morning meeting to begin. It never does.

I've wrestled with whether to return to a regular job ever since I resigned in January 2021, and my subconscious dream-state knows it.

It's been eighteen months now. Shortly before we left on vacation, I accepted an almost-full-time job at the university I left in 2014. When I return home from the trip, I will start the new job that's kind of the same as my old job, working as the administrative coordinator for the MFA program, the undergraduate honors program, and another master's program on campus.

If I were to sit down with a dream interpreter to explain the bacon-bear-conference-center dream, I suspect she would say I'm anxious about the unknowns waiting for me at a regular job after so much time away. Maybe the grizzly bear is a manifestation of my anxiety. Maybe the grizzly bear symbolizes my long-COVID symptoms, the monster that's hiding underneath the mask. Maybe the grizzly bear is a warning of some kind.

That's all well and good, dream analyst, but what does the bacon mean?! What about the *bacon?!*

My bear-haunted work dream rose and evaporated with the juniper-infused morning dew in the Shoshone valley. I woke before the sunrise. There in the valley of Douglas fir and juniper, I slept as well as one can sandwiched between two gangly boys on inch-thick sleeping mats in sleeping bags, which is to say hardly at all. Our gray air mattress had inflated and then quickly deflated before anyone could sleep on it, so we used it as a tarp to hold our muddy shoes at the entrance of our tent and shared the two sleeping mats we brought. Between the three a.m. bear patrol and my predawn wake-up, I must have slept five hours. It's a far cry from my usual eight or nine, but no big deal.

It would be fine.

It would be fine, because we were nestled in a small valley between a mountain and the Shoshone River, no bears had eaten us overnight, the whole world was fragrant with what I kept saying was juniper and sage, the only sound was water rushing, and today was the day we'd enter Yellowstone!

Yellowstone, the place I accidentally kept calling Jellystone! Jellystone, the land of Yogi Bear, Huckleberry Hound, and stolen pic-a-nic baskets.

Gasp! Maybe it was Yogi Bear *in my dream!*

This Jellystone-Yellowstone trip up could be a looming long-COVID brain glitch or residue leftover from camping with my parents at Jellystone Park a couple nights ago. I'm not sure, but either way, I laughed every time I used the wrong word while both boys tossed out an annoyed, "Mom!" and rolled their eyes.

Most things about my long-COVID journey seemed mostly healed by the time we reached Jelly-I-mean-Yellowstone. Mostly. I had felt so proud of my body throughout our visit to the Badlands. It was *so hot* and yet I didn't overheat. Over the last year and a half, I had learned to listen for the signs of a POTS attack. Fatigue usually came first, quickly followed by a headache. If I listened, I could cut it off at the pass with lots of Liquid I.V. and rest—a short nap, or even just a small break to sit and put up my feet.

POTS (or Postural Orthostatic Tachycardia Syndrome) is a dysautonomia, meaning a disorder of the autonomic nervous system. Your autonomic nervous system controls all of the functions in your body that happen automatically, without you needing to think consciously about them. This includes your heart rate, your blood pressure, your breathing, your temperature gauges, and so on. Some people with POTS have trouble getting out of bed because their condition is so debilitating.

I am one of the lucky ones—my condition seems relatively mild and manageable. Sometimes I get dizzy. Sometimes I can't stoop down quickly or turn around to untangle my dog's leash when she wraps herself around me. Sometimes I get brain fog that clogs the lane between the words in my head and my tongue, and I struggle to finish a sentence, wondering where it went. Sometimes my head hurts and I'm so tired I just need to go lie down for a little while.

Over the last eighteen months, I've designed my life to accommodate these symptoms, so it seems to me that I should be able to do normal things now, like stand up and walk around for hours at a time, spin around in a circle without getting dizzy, use the right word in a sentence, or type the right homonym in a paragraph. (I just started to type "write" instead of "right." This happens *all of the time* now and is the most humiliating lingering symptom of my long-COVID journey. I am a *writer*. How can I not use the right "right"?!)

But by two o'clock in Yellowstone, my body let me know it was not up for this adventure anymore. We'd made it through most of the east side of Yellowstone, gawking and "wow"-ing around every turn and scenic overlook, peeking over the edge of the Upper and Lower Falls, staring down a bison as it wandered across the road, spying some kind of deer or elk or something in the trees near our picnic table, and squinting far into the distance across a green valley to where people *swore* there were wolves.

I wasn't the only one losing it. On the heels of his medicine withdrawal, Elvis melted down first. Then Henry got a stomachache, and finally it was my turn.

FIVE HOURS IN A TENT WITH TEENAGERS IS NOT ENOUGH SLEEP, YOU MORON. WHY ARE YOU DOING THIS TO US! My brain screamed from behind my left eyeball as I navigated us out of Jellystone . . . Yellowstone. I drove through the red haze of pain to the McCrea Bridge Campground in Caribou-Targhee National Forest, Idaho. My brain kept on screaming while we set up camp. It yelled so much I could hardly hear the pirate volunteer camp host tell us there wasn't electricity. Battered yet undeterred, my brain mewed and whined while I couldn't get the fire started.

I flopped down in the double seat camp chair with its rusty bolts and cried, "I don't want to eat peanut butter and jelly again!" So I booked a roadside cabin and initiated the McCrea Wells Campsite Teardown.

"Don't get your hopes up," I said to the boys. "Who knows what we've signed up for."

My head kept pounding as we drove up to the cabin park situated on the side of the road in front of Henry's Fork ("Hey! Henry! It's your fork!"), right next to a gas station. I checked in and got our keys. There were *beds*. And *air-conditioning*. And a *shower*. And *electricity*.

"We're never tent camping again," I told the boys.

"Yeah!" They shouted with glee, carrying their electronics into the cabin and nestling into their bed.

I dragged myself to the camp store next to the cabins to buy butter, cheese, and more bread. We were most definitely not eating peanut butter and jelly tonight! After a long, glorious shower and transfer into some cozy pajamas, I plugged in the skillet *and it worked. Just like that.* As the butter sizzled on the griddle, the savory aroma of melting cheddar and toasted bread filled the cabin, and the angels sang, holy, holy, holy is the Lord Almighty, the whole earth is full of his gluten, and his dairy, and his glory.

POTS Attack in Yellowstone

A thousand-year flood has washed away
    the soil around my nerves.
Frayed, they dangle, hiss, and flicker
    like live wire radiating
behind my eyes, a pulsating pressure
    of geysers at the potter's pit
or is it painter's pot I forgot there are limits
    to our existence limits
to how far I can go before
    the earth gives way to pain,
I mean rain, Earth and me, together
    we have collectively given in,
up, over, whatever. 3,500 square miles
    to discover but we are driving
away midday. The seismic activity
    in this truck propels us
west or south or was it a loop why
    does it feel like we've been
here before, just another volcanic
    hot spot, one more before
the exit, sections of my brain shut down
    for repair after whole houses

washed downstream, Earth and I,
have lost our worlds
and our words are everything.

The next morning, I woke up from eight dreamless hours of sleep refreshed and ready to tackle another full day in Yellowstone.

Did you know that Americans average 5.5 hours of sleep these days? Pre-electricity, people tended to get 9.5 hours a night, interrupted by a brief wakeup midway through to do some household chores or other "intimate" activities. It's called "biphasic sleep."

Pre-COVID, I probably averaged seven hours of sleep. It seemed like enough, and maybe it was. But after COVID? I couldn't sleep enough. On a regular workday, I would wake up at seven, drag myself through the morning Liquid I.V. and coffee routine, lead a Zoom-based strategy session, wrap up with a migraine, make a meal like a zombie, fall asleep on the couch at seven p.m., wake up to go to bed at nine p.m., sleep a deep and dreamless ten hours, and start the process over again the following morning. Resigning allowed me ten hours of sleep every night plus a two- to three-hour nap midafternoon. I had to sleep that much. I had no other choice.

It's been eighteen months since then, though. Most days, I sleep from nine p.m. until six thirty a.m. My walks are leisurely strolls through our neighborhood. I spend no more than an hour at a time sitting at my computer before taking a break.

So why was I surprised by the Yellowstone POTS attack?

It was early in the pandemic when I first got sick with COVID. Brandon and I had low-grade fevers and fatigue for two weeks, me with shortness of breath that was enough to consider going to the hospital but not enough to feel like I might die. Tests were in short supply and reserved for the very sick, so we were told to assume it was COVID based on our symptoms and seek emergency care if it got worse.

Thankfully, it didn't get worse. We regained energy and began living like everyone else under new stay-at-home orders. While taking our walks, I struggled to talk and walk simultaneously and had to stop to catch my breath. Then other symptoms started—rapid heart rate and chest pains and lung pain that persisted for weeks, constant thirst, dry throat, fatigue. Then the tingling in my hands and feet started along with numbness in my face, daily headaches, dizziness, brain fog, excessive sweating, purple toes, forgetting words, and swapping terms without realizing the slip.

My healthcare provider gratefully took my complaints seriously and ordered test after test, the expense of which I knew would have been high if it wasn't for our great insurance. Before COVID, I saw a doctor for my annual physical and that was it. But in 2020, I saw a neurologist and a cardiologist and a pulmonologist. Soon, I'd add in a neurological physical therapist. When I finally got a diagnosis for what had been happening for six months, I felt relief and grief. Relief that someone could finally validate that what I was experiencing wasn't all in my head, and grief that the life I had known and the energy I once had seemed to be gone. Life as I knew it would forever be different.

According to an article from Yale Medicine, long-COVID affects somewhere between 5 to 30 percent of people who get COVID-19.[1] A lot of people have developed and experienced post-acute COVID-19 syndrome (the medical term for long-COVID), but early in the pandemic I didn't know anyone else who had experienced the same confusing symptoms, and many of the physicians I saw were just as baffled as I was. Living in a small town that denied COVID was even a thing amplified my feelings of isolation. I joined long-COVID, POTS, and Dysautonomia International support groups on Facebook and marveled at this emerging community of people who were all experiencing varying degrees of mysterious symptoms somehow linked to the pandemic. Their stories ranged from accounts of annoying doctors who denied they were experiencing anything ("It's all in your head")

---

1 "Long COVID (Post-COVID Conditions, PCC)," Yale Medicine, https://www.yalemedicine.org/conditions/long-covid-post-covid-conditions-pcc.

to heartbreaking stories of lives, careers, and relationships lost because of this confounding condition.

For me, it helped to learn the source of my mysterious symptoms and to put a name to my chronic illness—it gave me hope and steps to take on the long, slow journey to recovery, building up endurance and strength to live with POTS.

"What you're describing just sounds like getting old," one neurologist told me. "People are dying of COVID in hospitals. What you're describing doesn't sound like you were that sick." He got COVID shortly after that virtual appointment, and part of me hoped he got long-COVID so that God might instill a little more empathy in his cold, judgy heart. I didn't want him to die. I just wanted him to get sick *enough*. Doctors like that neurologist sowed seeds of doubt in my mind. Maybe I wasn't sick? Maybe I was just getting old? Is this what it feels like to be on the verge of forty? Am I destined to be tired and dizzy and foggy all of the time? Maybe these are the limits of a finite life.

On September 19, 2020, I wrote on my blog about my diagnosis:

> I want to take long hikes, walk a nine-hole golf
> course, explore parks, and bike ride with my family
> again without feeling like my heart or head is going
> to explode or collapsing in exhaustion at the end of
> the day. I believe I can get there, but also maybe I
> won't. Maybe I will be the other half of adults who
> develop POTS as a result of a viral infection who
> do not recover to their normal lives after five years.
> And that is okay too. This quiet space with hard
> constraints that insist on rest is holy, sacred room
> to be in the presence of the One I fear and love,
> and to receive the comfort of the Holy Spirit. I am
> surrounded by those I love. I have all that I need. Joy
> and gratitude pepper my days. There is hope that,
> no matter what, *all shall be well, all shall be well, all
> manner of things shall be well.*

(Me and Julian of Norwich are besties now.)

It's been almost two years since I got that diagnosis. It's hard to recall what "normal" looked like before March 2020. I sometimes remember charging forth into every day with deep wells of ambition, staying up late into the night writing or working on a project, leading meetings at Spire, spending so much of the day *thinking* . . . it all seems so full and fast-paced and impossible now, still. Even though over the last two years I have experienced recovery and healing, progress I'm so grateful for, I keep wanting to be fully recovered and even sometimes believe that I *am* fully recovered until my body reminds me that I am not. It has limits.

Last December, just over a year after my initial diagnosis, I saw a neurological physical therapist for the first time. She spent ninety minutes with me sharing about the cranial nerve and patterns doctors who deal with dizziness are seeing in long-COVID patients. She talked about the brain stem and the neck and walked through the many and varied wonky symptoms I'd experienced. She gave me an exercise that involved shaking my head yes and no for one minute each, focusing on a spot on the wall during that time.

"Do this twice a day at 80 beats per minute until this seems stupidly easy, and then slowly increase to 120 bpm. Don't push it," she warned. "We don't want you to trigger another forty-five-day headache."

Shaking your head yes or no shouldn't be an issue, but I had carried my head around nervously for the last year and a half, careful to keep steady and avoid the destabilizing feeling of being on a boat when I wasn't. I shouldn't have to think about how to shake my head, or if to. Sometimes I felt like I moved like a ninety-year-old.

Even though I was grateful that I seemed to be recovering, the wells of energy seemed to stay full longer, and my physical endurance was improving, my brain was not done healing. I woke up the morning after the shaking-the-head exercise with a pounding headache and that slow-brain feeling. It was discouraging. I overdid it with the nodding and an evening holiday gathering. To make up for that energy deficit I needed to give my brain more space to rest, again.

Neurological healing and recovery take a long time. I don't have brain fog anymore, most of the time. I don't need to nap every single day, just every few days, especially if I've been active, talking to people for several hours in a row, and standing. Performing any complex activity that involves using multiple senses and areas of my brain simultaneously still wears me out in ways it never did before, provoking headaches and brain fog and exhaustion. My brain doesn't get as exhausted as it did in the final months of my job, when trying to run a strategy session sunk me into massive and weeks-long migraines. The headaches are smaller now, warning signals from my sweet, terrified brain to take a break and rest.

So that is what I've tried to do: take breaks and rest.

Until this trip.

Neurological issues and autonomic nervous system disorders are private struggles. There's no cast or crutch or cane that signals *I'm still quite sick actually*. This is a strange space in which to operate, because I love the life I have now, but it is not the life I had pre-COVID. You can grieve the life you lost and also be grateful for the life you gained. You can hold both truths in your hands. Isn't that the reality of loss, no matter what it is you've lost? I miss the team I led at Spire. I miss being a leader and a problem solver, a strategist and a creative thinker. I miss this part of me, the part that is handicapped now by damaged nerve endings, the part I am aware may never be fully restored.

But I also love the life I have now and am grateful for the space and flexibility to rest, to write, to cook, to walk, to be with my family, to observe the natural world around me, to appreciate silence and slowness, to dwell and linger in God's peace and quiet, to revel in it in ways the busy life I led before did not permit. There's so much space, here, now.

I think this is what we are called to do, to go on living in the capacity that we are given, even if our world is smaller or feels insignificant. It isn't. I am worthy and valued because I *am*. That's it. No performance review or checked-off list is required to validate the importance of our existence. Just being is enough. And out of that worthiness pours gratitude for every single falling snowflake, every single whispered "me too" of shared experience, every single shared smile or tear.

On the way back into Yellowstone after our long night's sleep, Henry listed off the animals we had and hadn't yet seen on the cute coloring sheet the park ranger gave us when we arrived. Bears were still on the list, thank God.

"Can you believe that people come into Yellowstone and literally ask what time they let the animals out?" I told Henry. Our camp guide Walt had shared that little tidbit with us.

"Like it's a zoo!"

"That's hilarious," I replied.

"I'm really gonna miss Yellowstone," he said.

"Me too."

Before we left the cabin, I did a quick search for trails to hike and found a 3.5-mile loop trail to a waterfall. I love waterfalls. One of my fondest memories from when we went out west when I was sixteen included a quick poke to see Yosemite Falls. Other tourists were climbing on rocks to get closer to the water, but I watched from the bridge as my brothers tried to maneuver across the boulders until my parents called them back and away.

Now I wanted *that*, the thrill of shivering and lunging for the next granite slab that got you that much closer to the rushing river. A step off the beaten path. A challenge that we could take. A victory we could win. We planned to take the Biscuit Basin Trail that followed the Little Firehole River to the Mystic Falls Trail, to Mystic Falls itself, then loop up to Fairy Creek Trail, then around to the overlook, then zigzag back down to Biscuit Basin.

It looked like a challenge, but I believed it was one that we could complete. I failed to figure out exactly where the trail began before we left the cabin and took us on an hour-long back-and-forth detour before we finally arrived at Biscuit Basin. It was the first volcanic hot spring any of us had seen, so we walked in awe along the boardwalk toward the trailhead, watching the surface of the earth bubble and steam. As we entered the trail, a sign let us know that bear activity was reported in the area last on July 14 . . . three days ago. *Maybe the grizzly in my dream was a warning!*

Henry had his walking stick and a CamelBak, and I had a backpack with a bladder thing too, as well as our bug spray, lunches, Elvis's water bottle, and our bear spray . . . of course. We walked along the river until the trail of dirt became rocks, and then we followed the rest of the hikers in taking off our boots and socks, rolling up our shorts, and climbing toward the waterfall. Elvis hung back, hanging onto our boots and socks while Henry and I crept closer to the roar. All along the edges were hot springs that trickled into the river. We got as near as we felt like we could get without wading up to our shorts, gasping and laughing and feeling like kings and queens. After, the three of us continued our climb up the trail, stopping to breathe and drink water, shouting, "Hey bear! How ya doing?" every few minutes to make sure grizzlies knew we were around.

We climbed 606 feet up from Biscuit Basin to the top of the mountain—less than half the height of the Empire State Building. The wooded trail was thick with evergreens and silent, eerily quiet. We encountered no bears, just chipmunks, squirrels, mosquitoes, monarchs, birds, perhaps an eagle, and carpenter ants at work to decompose a fallen burnt tree.

Amid all of the grandeur and largeness of Yellowstone, it's easy to overlook the smallest things that are doing important, behind-the-scenes work. My healing has been like that—microscopic cells busy doing long, important, behind-the-scenes work. I used to move so much faster through the woods. When you're in a rush to just finish a hike so you can say that you did it, these are the moments you can miss: the universe of creatures taking care of creation on a small patch of land in a forest filled with even more universes.

I'm grateful for the slow way. I don't want to miss the carpenter ants anymore.

It took us far longer than the anticipated hour and thirty-eight minutes estimated on AllTrails.com—I think we spent more like three hours on the trail—but we stopped a lot, and we climbed into that waterfall, and I didn't have another POTS attack.

I didn't have another POTS attack. This amazes me. We hiked one trail in this massive park. One. It was 3.5 miles long. I didn't die from exhaustion. I didn't develop a headache. No one complained. It was 3.5 whole miles long and only 3.5 miles long. There are over 1,100 miles of hiking trails weaving throughout the 3,472 square miles of Yellowstone National Park. There's so much more to see and experience and witness, so much more that is so much grander and larger than I am. And also, I didn't have a POTS attack.

After our hike, we waited with hundreds of other travelers until Old Faithful faithfully burst from the earth, a slow-building gush like a water main break and then a hundred-foot spray heavenward for not just seconds but minutes of white water misting the surrounding landscape. I persuaded the boys to wait until it was over with a promise to visit the gift shop after, and then we made our way to the places we'd left for last, beginning with the Grand Prismatic Pool and then Artists' Paint Pots.

Henry and I surveyed the palette of teal, purple, orange, and pink mud pots bubbling and were sure there were bear prints in the steaming pools of acidic water and rock. I didn't have to use my bear spray. As the two of us walked back to the car from the paint pots, I told Henry how glad I was that he wanted to keep going to see the last few things on our list.

"If there's ever a question about whether to do something, the answer is probably yes," I said. "Especially in Yellowstone."

"Yeah," Henry replied. "There's nothing here that's not worth it."

We said "wow" a lot. A lot.

Elvis is my indoor boy. He usually gets his steps walking from his bedroom to the bathroom to the fridge and back again, so walking seven miles up and down a mountain was a little out of his normal rhythm. I watched him warily, wondering how this exertion might affect the rest of the day.

"Want to join us or opt out of this stop?" I asked him before Henry and I left the truck.

"I'll hang back here," he said, turning to his phone and turning up his playlist in the back seat.

Henry and I climbed up and down more stairs and hills to check out the otherworldly sites across Yellowstone. By the time we reached the Mammoth Hot Springs, a glacial-looking plateau of travertine formed from cooling calcium carbonate, the early evening light angled through the trees and started to cast long, stark shadows across the landscape. My knee started to hurt on the stairs up, but Henry and I made our final climb to catch a better view of Mammoth Hot Springs. I kept thinking the monument itself would be cold and malleable, like a mound of snow plowed to clear the driveway back home, but no. Travertine is hard, durable stone.

By the time we started our descent off the travertine terrace, hardly anyone else was around. How is the entire world not flocking to this place, this unusual, baffling landscape with surprises tucked in every single overlook? We drove along deserted Upper Terrace Drive, seeing one or two other travelers, then turned left again.

Despite the previous day's POTS threats, I wasn't ready to be done with Yellowstone. We took the roads less traveled north as far as we could, stopping in Mammoth for dinner, but nothing was open. I slowed the truck to a crawl so we could gawk at the deer grazing in Fort Yellowstone. The north part of the park was still closed after a thousand-year flood washed away and permanently changed the wild, extreme landscape of the northeast corner of Yellowstone just a month before our trip, but still we drove along the steep banks, eager to take in more and more of what stretched vast and uncontainable all around us.

There was a time in my life, before COVID, when taking three weeks to travel the country and visit bubbling geysers and endless forested mountain ranges would have seemed indulgent and irresponsible. Isn't it enough to sit down on the sofa in the evening, turn on National Geographic, and let the paid videographers deliver footage of these unfamiliar lands in our backyard? I had strategy sessions to lead! I had conferences to attend! I suspect there are lots of me out there, unable or unwilling to venture beyond the known places.

But on this side of the pandemic, on this side of my struggle with POTS, time is so *limited*, and there is so much abundance beyond my backyard. Why have I waited so long to carve out these expeditions? Why did it take a landslide of epic proportions in my own life to compel me to find the long hikes that lead us nowhere and everywhere? Why did it take being so sick to want to live well?

The terrain across Yellowstone did not become what it is without strife; in fact, it is only magnificent because of heat and friction, wind and water, chaos and time. Perhaps all things require this cycle of generation, disintegration, and rebirth to be real, true, good, and beautiful.

A double rainbow appeared in the sky as the sun descended in the west, its presence only possible because of living water somewhere in the atmosphere. Elvis turned on "Life's a Happy Song" from *The Muppets Movie*, and I thought to myself, yes it is. *Weeping may stay for the night, but rejoicing comes in the morning.*[2] We finished the day with over 23,000 steps, tired, free of bears and POTS symptoms, and so, so, so happy to be sleeping in real beds again.

I crawled under the covers and sighed. Life's a happy song.

There's nothing here that's not worth it.

---

2 Psalm 30:5.

Hiking Trails Above Dormant Volcanoes

for my son, Elvis, in Yellowstone National Park

When the wild world we enter splashes
against the boulders, you're the last to trespass
and opt instead to watch us take our chances,
holding our boots and socks in your dry hands.
This is how it's been with you since birth—
a constant hum electric buzzes warnings
for all the real and imagined fears on Earth
that keep your feet from sprouting wings.
Miles of hiking later, we are where
the eagles soar. Adrenaline propels
you toward the edge. I see empty air,
imagine you leaping. Instead you smile.
We're high, and free, our hearts alive out here,
but wolves and bears, they could be anywhere.

Chapter 6

Abiding the Wilderness

The next leg of our trip had one purpose: get us from one place to the next. We'd leave Yellowstone for a conference we'd be attending in Boise. If we saw anything of interest, it would be through the bug-smeared windshield of our blue Ford F-150 as we hit highway cruising speed straight on 'til Boise.

We slept until I woke up without my alarm, packed the truck, said goodbye to our Cabin Village refuge in Island Park, Idaho, and headed west. The Grand Tetons would have to be checked off our list of national parks another day.

"Today's all about just getting to Boise," I told the boys. "We'll stop for PB&J at a rest stop along the way."

"Hey!" I realized with a start. "Today's the *last day for peanut butter and jelly!* The rest of the trip, we're back to real human food from *restaurants* and *grocery stores*." I cranked up the soundtrack to *Hamilton* as we headed west, belting out with happy tears in my eyes, "How lucky we are to be alive right now!" feeling every word, content to see nothing interesting for the next three hundred and fifty miles.

The terrain opened up as we left the Rocky Mountains and drove through Idaho Falls along US-20. Trees became few and far between until there were hardly any, just a few rolling hills covered in dried grass and then flat land. Very, very flat land.

This stretch of emptiness between the mountains and Boise is virtually uninhabitable by humans. Sustained winds of 35 mph and regular gusts nearly knocked us off our feet when we stopped to use the restroom. We leaned into the hot wind for a hot minute. Looking around as we drove, so much of the landscape felt useless. It's all empty space you just need to cross to get from here to there.

That's the wilderness for you.

On a whim one afternoon eight years ago in 2014, following a particularly difficult meeting with my boss, I applied for jobs, any job, really, that might take me away from the job I had been in for the last seven years. As much as I loved my little office, my role as the MFA program's administrative director, serving at the university where I'd earned my bachelor's and master's, I'd had enough. I was tired of feeling like I could never advance beyond my existing position. I wanted to quit everything, even our little house on Morgan parallel with the wide open spaces of Freer Field, our church family and close friends all within walking distance, and the community that held all of that in its polite, Midwestern embrace. I wanted to quit everything. It happens sometimes, one or two or three strong gales that ask us to bend and bend and bend until we're brittle from the effort of holding so much together. It doesn't matter how much good we had, the bad is enough bad to need to flee.

But days rolled over, the gales slowed, I forgot about all of the resumes I'd sent, and I settled back into the comfort of the known routine. When the phone rang months later with an apology for the delay and an invitation to interview—would I still be interested?—I questioned whether I was still interested. Things weren't so bad. My boss was on sabbatical. I valued that temporary autonomy, aware it would vanish as soon as he returned, but with him away for several months, I could manage the journal, the press, and the program the way I liked. I went to the interview anyway, for practice, to dust the rust off of having conversations about my strengths and weaknesses and experiences.

It was easy, stress-free; I wasn't looking anymore. What was the harm in just talking?

Six short weeks later there was a for sale sign in front of our home. The job was mine, notice given, and plans made to relocate from Ashland, Ohio, to Akron, Ohio, a closer commute to the east side of Cleveland where I'd serve as managing editor in the marketing office of a business school. Just like that, we said goodbye to the home and community we'd spent seven years building.

The years leading up to this move were filled with rocky and challenging terrain, and I was tired from all of that exertion. Besides the deteriorating relationship with my boss, Brandon's work schedule sent him out of town weekly, leaving me home with a full-time job and three children under the age of nine. My mom had just been diagnosed with kidney cancer. For one very long year, I had wrestled privately with a colleague's advances and the inner turmoil of emotions—revulsion, flattery, anxiety, and confusion—that churned in me. In between his comments and attention, I wondered, Had I somehow asked for this advance? Did I *want* his attention? What was this desire to be desired, and where did it come from, and wasn't my husband's love *enough*? I spent a whole book trying to figure this out.[3]

In the wake of that mess, I questioned every other man's behavior around me. I didn't know that starting a new job and moving away would feel like a victory. *Yes! We will be free from the toxicity of this life! We will be closer to my parents and to Brandon's parents! We will leave all of this and be well again.*

In the Bible, when Elijah stood up to Jezebel and the Baal worshippers, I imagine he felt like me in the days after I accepted a new job. He proved to them that his God was real, ever-present, and powerful in the midst of both storm and silence. He stood up to the people who were in power. He stepped out from under their reign and exercised his free will with courage and might. He should've beat his chest and shouted, "I AM ELIJAH!!!!"

---

3 My memoir *American Honey: A Field Guide to Resisting Temptation*, published in 2021.

Instead the king threatened to kill him, and he ran for his life to the wilderness. After all God did in front of Jezebel's prophets, I can see Elijah cowering in caves all day, waiting for someone to come and kill him. The victories didn't matter. The threats—real or perceived—persisted, haunting his waking and sleeping.

That's what trauma—even mild trauma—does to you; it sets your nerves on fire and places your entire body on alert. You don't leave behind trauma. It's like static electricity. The more you try to calm it, the more amped it gets until your hair is standing up straight and you can't get your sweater unglued from your side.

It takes time and space and rest to heal the brittleness. It takes wilderness.

My extended family has a small farm in Ohio. It is mostly agricultural fields that taper off into woods that descend into a swampy valley carved through by a shallow creek. I spent a lot of summers as a child wandering through the forest and wading in the cool, clear water with my cousins.

I have a distinct memory of my grandmother designating the swamp as protected land, land that could never be developed, but when I asked my mom to verify that information, she was certain that never happened.

"The swamp used to be a pasture," she told me. "Grandpa used to take the cows down there."

I was disappointed in this misremembering. My grandma loved the national parks and took many trips with her husband and kids to visit historical places. She had a couple chunks of petrified wood I marveled at tucked away in her living room's built-in oak cabinets. For years I have held this gem about my grandmother's environmental advocacy close to my chest, but now, I'm no longer sure whether I inherited my passion to protect the land from my grandmother or whether I just projected it onto her memory. It doesn't have to be either/or. Maybe it's both—beauty and function, conservation and survival.

My family has talked about draining the swamp and bringing back the lower pastureland, turning it back into usable property for a couple more cows, most likely. In the eyes of the economy, swampland looks like wasteland.

But I know the value of that land. Riparian zones are places along the edges of waterways where forest meets swamp and swamp meets creek. There in the riparian zone, some of the most dynamic and rich biodiversity exists. Swamps purify water and provide habitat for the native creatures that have been living there for thousands of years and centuries before us Europeans arrived. It's these behind-the-scenes ecosystems that are easy to write off as useless, except our continued existence depends upon them. The swamp is a small strip of land on our sixty-four-acre farm, and yet it is essential, vital, serving so many unseen and unacknowledged purposes besides potential grazing land for cattle.

Wildernesses like my family's swamp and the deserts and grass-lands just west of Yellowstone might appear to be useless for humans, or useful only to desecrate with nuclear testing, but in God's peaceable kingdom, wildernesses like these barren places are vital to our planet's survival.

The trouble is, it's hard to see the beauty of the wilderness when you're sinking in the muck and mire.

It had been just three weeks since we moved and I started my new job. The job itself wasn't stressful, but the commute was longer than I imagined, usually over an hour each way with a fifteen-minute walk from the parking garage to my office. I left the house in the dark and I came home in the dark.

Anything I used to help Brandon with around the house and for the most part enjoyed doing—cooking dinner, reading with the kids, folding laundry—had become a chore. And the things I *really* enjoyed doing—reading, writing, gardening, drinking a glass of wine with my friends—felt gone forever. My friends were in Ashland. My writing time evaporated. There was no space for words.

"I have to do everything and there's no time for anything," I thought . . . or maybe I said it out loud, accenting the words with every piece of clothing pulled from the washer and flung into the dryer.

When I am stressed, I don't shed responsibilities. I take them all on. No one else does anything; I must do everything. No one appreciates me; I will prove my worth. I am the martyr, and oh, how I've been martyred.

As each piece of laundry thumped and dinked in wet clumps of denim and zippers, Brandon watched TV in the living room. I fumed.

"You know," he said over the din of some sportsing, "I can take care of the laundry tomorrow. You don't have to do that." He was probably eating nachos or something too, I bet.

I flung the final damp pants into the dryer and slammed the door, then scooped the basket of cold, dry, and wrinkled clothes up to my hip to be folded. *No, this is my life now. I will do all of the things, even if you offer to do some of them. It's what martyrs do.*

Wilderness can be physical, emotional, relational, intellectual, or spiritual. It is the empty stretch of land that follows the mountaintop highs and valley lows of births and deaths, marriages and divorces, moves and promotions, graduation and retirement. After the rush or crash spans a vast emptiness of *what now*. Whether you're holding a trophy or the shattered remains of some great thing you counted precious, you're holding it with no shelf to rest it on, no next step, no dust pan to sweep it up. Whatever wilderness it is, it can be ruthless. It can feel pointless. It can make every decision you made to get to this stage feel like a throbbing mistake.

One year into our move that was supposed to mark victory, I wondered if it might be easier for Brandon and me to just separate. We were right in the middle of mile marker 13, the year of Brandon's farewell tour, the "write a better story" year. The changes we had made in the last year meant more time away from each other, more time with Brandon on the road. When he was home, he was angry. When he was gone, I felt relieved. Long silences and text conversations like air traffic control filled the space between us—*when are you coming home?, making (soggy) Crock-Pot chicken for dinner, we need more shredded cheese, Elvis is throwing a tantrum again, be home at nine.* In between those text messages, I wanted to scream, *Don't you love me? Why don't you adore me? When are you coming* home *to me?*

"It's worse than anything we've been through before," I lamented to a friend. "Before, when I felt sad or angry or lonely, he responded with frustration, compassion, or intimacy. Now, he just doesn't care."

If he didn't care, then I wouldn't either.

They were building new apartments within walking distance of my office in Cleveland. Every day I passed them at the end of my hour-long commute from our home in West Akron. *I could move there, I could make a life.* I imagined what it might be like, to be separate and be on my own. I made good enough money. Our debt burden was manageable. We had two cars. The kids could stay with him during the week and see me on the weekends. It would not be so bad. It would not be so hard. I passed more cars and bridges and construction, and I imagined cars veering into my lane, my lane ending and my car colliding with the concrete barrier. *What would it feel like, all that collision? What would it be like, that free fall into the valley?*

Stop it. Look back to the road ahead. Look ahead.

One year in, and I still hadn't found a routine for writing or reading or cooking or gardening or anything else I used to enjoy doing. My job was great, the kids were great, their schools were great, our neighborhood was great, but I wasn't great. Brandon and I weren't great. My mom's health worsened.

At the start of his journey into the wilderness, Elijah was ready to die. "I have had enough, Lord," he said. "Take my life; I am no better than my ancestors."

> All at once an angel touched him and said, "Get up and eat." He looked around, and there by his head

was some bread baked over hot coals, and a jar of
water. He ate and drank and then lay down again.
The angel of the Lord came back a second time
and touched him and said, "Get up and eat, for the
journey is too much for you." So he got up and ate
and drank. Strengthened by that food, he traveled
forty days and forty nights until he reached Horeb,
the mountain of God. There he went into a cave
and spent the night.[4]

Get up and eat, for the journey is too much for you. The journey
is too much. Just eat. Just drink. Just keep walking. And when you are
ready, you'll arrive at the mountain of God. You might not know that's
where you're heading, but keep walking.

Despite the vast expanse of land I've witnessed and explored with
my children as we've crossed the country, wilderness around the globe
and in the States is disappearing rapidly. From 2001 to 2017, the non-
profit Conservation Science Partners (CSP) found that "the United
States lost more than a football field's worth of natural area to devel-
opment every 30 seconds."[5] That's eight football fields in the time it
takes me to brew a cup of tea, a total of 24 million acres in sixteen
years . . . or nine Grand Canyons, the equivalent of almost one-third
the land in all of our national parks.[6]

This loss of land began to draw the attention of leaders as far
back as the late 1800s, when the United States Congress established
the first national park, Yellowstone. Today there are 433 national park

4 1 Kings 19:4–9.
5 "Methods and Approach Used to Estimate the Loss and Fragmentation of Natural Lands in the Conterminous U.S. from 2001 to 2017," Conservation Science
Partners, 17 October 2019, https://www.csp-inc.org/public/CSP_Disappearing_
US_Tech_Report_v101719.pdf.
6 Valerie Volcovici, "U.S. Has Lost 24 Million Acres of Natural Land in 16 Years:
Independent Report," Reuters, https://www.reuters.com/article/
idUSKCN1UW08Y/.

sites in the United States and its territories, spanning more than 85 million acres.[7] But between 1982 and 2003, the United States added 35 million acres of developed land and is projected to add over 54 million more by 2030, which dramatically impacts the immediate and surrounding ecosystems.[8]

We literally have no margin for wilderness, in our country or in our lives. Things need space to grow and unfold in their own time, relatively unaffected by us. But we affect everything.

In the spring of that first year in Akron, I began to notice a heron on my morning commute, perched upon a fallen log that extended out into the reservoir I crossed. Its profile was dark against the early morning muted light that made the woods, the water, the fog, and the road monochrome. Every morning I slowed to scan the edges of the water in case it was somewhere other than the limb I'd grown accustomed to spotting him.

"It" became a "he." He was there so consistently that I worried when I didn't see him—why had he left, when would he return, why did he stay at this particular reservoir, why always on the same log, what if he disappeared forever? I probed the heron with questions long after I had passed his perch, all along the highway, my heron in the passenger seat.

The heron became a mirror, a companion, and an antagonist. I loved his consistency and even his sudden absence some mornings when I looked but didn't see. *Where'd you go, you silly bird?* I asked. I pointed out the heron to my daughter one evening—*Look, look, the great blue heron!*— too fast and too late for her to glimpse the camouflaged bird in shadow. I wanted her to also hope in things unseen and seen.

---

7 "About Us," National Park Service, https://www.nps.gov/aboutus/national-park-system.htm.

8 Eric M. White, Anita T. Morzillo, and Ralph J. Alig, "Past and projected rural land conversion in the US at state, regional, and national levels," Landscape and Urban Planning, 2009, https://research.fs.usda.gov/treesearch/35451.

On the morning we heard about the shooting in Charleston, South Carolina, there were two herons. One flew alongside my car as I passed and the other stood on the same log as always. One reflected my need for action, for response, for something to be done in this world or even to leave this world, and the other stood stalwart. Stubborn. Patient. I prayed to embody both.

Sometimes in the midst of all the motion and commotion, the back and forth of commutes and frenzy of movement, I felt like I was standing still, forever in the same place, like the heron.

Sometimes the monotony of my daily routine left me muttering with the Teacher in Ecclesiastes, "Meaningless! Meaningless! Utterly meaningless! Everything is meaningless." But as the weeks passed, I noticed the changing of the leaves and the hardening of the water, and then the shift from shades of gray to greens and browns, seemingly overnight. The ice with its animal footprints melted and merged back into the river. The heron left, and then the heron returned.

The earth tilted and turned and swayed and I turned with it, with the heron.

I used to believe in signs, like in that movie *Serendipity*, that fate or God slips clues into everyday life for us to notice and interpret to head in a particular direction. Sign, sign, everywhere a sign. These days, besides my heron, I see three twos everywhere—it's always 12:22 or 2:22 when I look. What does it all mean? I don't know. I don't know how to interpret the appearance of a heron or the way I notice certain groupings of numbers. Rather than directional signposts from heaven, I think they're more like notes left on a pillowcase by a spouse or a greeting card sent just because—small tokens of affection to remind us that He is here—God is here, present, available.

I look for God everywhere. During this particular season of seemingly changeless acceleration and deceleration, my heron was an icon of God's faithfulness, a sort of talisman that signaled presence, peace, and connection. He reminded me there are mysteries beyond the bounds of my intellect, that all fantasies I have of his ways and his thoughts are daydreams and anthropomorphic analogies. He reminded me that this is not my world to own. He reminded me that the meek shall inherit the earth, so love this earth now.

When I saw him and when I didn't, I kept the heron close.

During a wilderness season, weeks, months, maybe even years can pass by with us wondering what the heck we're doing here. The trophy collects dust, the shattered precious thing stays broken, it all seems to stay the same even though we keep waking up in the morning and going to sleep at night, pushing the hamster wheel through another round. Every little thing grates on our nerves, including and especially those closest in the fog.

I can't pinpoint a moment in the wilderness when Brandon and I found a new rhythm. No weekend retreat, big discussion in the kitchen, or whispered argument in the bedroom dissipated the malaise between us. One spring day after Brandon quit his job, he asked me to take a walk with him. We took Izzy, our little Westie, left the children to fend for themselves, and walked the square mile of our neighborhood. One walk turned into two, then three, then daily trips around the block. We walked and talked. We walked and didn't talk. We talked and laughed. We talked and disagreed and explained what made us angry and made jokes to break the tension and walked. We walked the same mile over and over and traveled farther, deeper, better, healthier.

The circumstances of our lives shifted. We shifted. I stopped dreaming about apartments on the east side of Cleveland. And when we made the decision to move back from Akron to Ashland, we brought those miles with us, walking out our lives around Williamsburg Court and Thomas Drive.

God told Elijah he was going to appear to him on the mountain of God, so Elijah went out to stand on the mountain. After the wind, after the earthquake, after the fire, then came the Lord, in the gentle whisper. *What are you doing here, Elijah?*

God was not in the wind or the earthquake or the fire. He was in the gentle whisper. *What are you doing here, Sarah? Why were you whipping wet laundry into the dryer at ten o'clock at night when you could be sitting with your husband watching sports, letting it sit for another twelve hours? Why the wet laundry frenzy? God is not there. God is in the gentle whisper: Come, sit. We'll take care of that tomorrow. Today had enough trouble of its own.*

This time in the wilderness might feel like nothing is happening, but *everything is happening here.*

It took countless days and nights for Elijah to move from exhaustion, starvation, and suicidal thoughts to be wooed toward the mountain of God. Then he traveled another forty days and nights to reach the mountain. When he got to the cave and God asked him, *What are you doing here?* Elijah ranted. He felt unseen. He felt unappreciated. He felt threatened. He felt abandoned. He felt alone. Even after the gentle whisper, even after God revealed himself to Elijah, when God asked him again, *What are you doing here?* Elijah repeated the exact same lament, as if to say, *That's great, God, thanks for showing up, but my circumstances haven't changed. I'm still trapped in this wilderness of fear, trauma, and abandonment. So what are you going to do about it?*

In Elijah's survival mode, God provided food and rest—just eat. Just drink. Just sleep. When Elijah was ready to take that journey again, God met him on the mountain. And when Elijah believed the lies that he was all alone and that everything depended upon him, God told him where he could find his friends, his allies, and his support to go back and do the work God called him to do. It took a lot of time, but God is patient. God is kind.

Some days, I long to climb to the top of a mountain and witness the work of God, to sit beside a rushing stream and feel the rising vapor, to stand and sweat on the precipice of a cliff that has been there for millions of years and will persist beyond the last blink and sigh of life on this planet. I long to seek out the wild places, because tucked in their ancient crevices is wonder and awe and contemplation, the seeds of love and empathy and action. I am here in this particular stretch of wilderness in Idaho to show my children, so they can show their children. I want them to listen. I want them to hear the voice calling in the wilderness, which is the wilderness, wooing, beckoning, enticing them deeper into communion with the One who has made all things.

That's why I have brought my boys into the physical wilderness, so that perhaps they might experience some of the awe and wonder I experience when we're in creation. Maybe when they find themselves lost in a spiritual wilderness, they will know there are places that remain where you can go and find refuge, mountains you can climb, raging rivers you can dip your toes in and find God.

That's all well and good, but Brandon and I didn't have a mountain to climb or an angel that fed us. We had a Westie that kept pace around our flat, paved, square mile, and I had a heron. During those two years I commuted to Cleveland followed by another year commuting to Ashland, I didn't have any margin to seek out a wilderness adventure. I woke up at 5:45 to eat and shower and drive to work to then drive home and eat and bathe my kids and go to sleep. When we moved back to Ashland so we could live in the same town where I worked again, I didn't reclaim those hours previously lost to commuting; I filled the days and hours to overflowing, all the way up until March 2020 when COVID hit and the world and my life changed entirely. Through the disorienting wilderness of my long-COVID limitations, I found God's answer to Elijah's lament—*Do not be afraid. I never left you. You are my beloved. You are never alone. You don't need to go anywhere or do anything in order to earn my love. Just be mine.*

God isn't just in the mountain or the thunder or the river or the rain, he's in the gentle whisper, right where you are.

God knows it might feel useless and meaningless, but *there is work being done in the wilderness.* There is strength being forged. There is confidence being built as all you depended upon outside of Love is stripped down. Gone is the fear, the anxiety, the responsibility, the busyness, the accomplishments. Instead, you rest in the mercy of the I Am, in the grace of God and the Love of Jesus Christ, in the hope of tomorrow.

Healing came in the wilderness. Strength returned. Space was made new. Not because we evacuated one place for another, but because we inhabited that place together.

It came through the slow plod of days, the slow working out of our salvation.

"See, I am doing a new thing! Now it springs up; do you not perceive it? I am making a way in the wilderness and streams in the wasteland."[9]

Trust me, and keep walking.

The landscape west of Idaho Falls and the Idaho National Laboratory churned over from windy, drought-dry grasslands to black-and-burnt orange, asphalt-looking mounds spotted by sagebrush shrubs. I didn't even know such a place existed.

"What happened here?" I wondered. *Was this the result of nuclear testing? Is this where the globe's used charcoal is discarded?*

We'd stumbled upon recent(-ish) cooled lava flows from volcanic eruptions that created Craters of the Moon, a national park in Idaho that extends for 1,100 square miles, roughly the size of Rhode Island. The charcoal and asphalt mounds formed during eight eruptive periods over the last 15,000 years and as recently as 2,100 years ago. The land had its last big belch just before the time of Christ. Even though the lava flows cooled a long time ago, the landscape is still sparse and rocky. Our good friends, the lichens, are hard at work transforming rock into habitable land, which can take thousands of years in Idaho's high desert climate.

But life persists even here. Tucked in between the lava crops, flows, and tubes is sagebrush, which provides respite for the desert creatures that call this place home. Mule deer, sage grouse, songbirds, pronghorns, and pikas—a distant relative of rabbits—have all found ways to adapt in the barren landscape.

---

9 Isaiah 43:19.

The first instruction to the people in Eden wasn't to be useful. No, God told them to be fruitful and multiply. Be fruitful. Bear fruit. Thousands of years later, Paul would tell the people that the defining fruit of the Spirit is love that manifests as joy, peace, patience, kindness, and a whole host of other bright berries that burst on your tongue.

Here in the Craters of the Moon Idaho desert, dwarf monkey flower, dwarf buckwheat, silver-leaved phacelia, and seven hundred other species are giving out their last blooms of summer before making the turn into August, multiplying joy, multiplying love, multiplying beauty in barren places, all for the sake of *being*.

Nothing *needed* to be created. Everything exists out of the gleeful, extravagant grace of God. The whole world is filled with fruitfulness.

That's all that God asks of us. Abide in the Vine. Acquiesce to pruning. Endure the wilderness.

Watch for the heron. Keep walking. Stay.

Look how much is growing, right here, in the middle of nowhere.

Craters of the Moon

This must be where they gather and harvest
charcoal for the planet's grills and dump
ground-up asphalt roads. Will it be like this
when the world ends? Instead of some
effervescent New Creation, Earth will vomit
burnt ends and overcooked chicken breasts,
leaving nothing but the consummate
mass of leftovers for any future guests.
But this is natural, not "disaster,"
simple fissure eruptions. Earth gave birth
here. Maybe there is hope in ashes.
All along apocalyptic edges,
purple dwarf monkey flowers bloom,
as if all things will really be made new.

Chapter 7

The Age of Beholding

—St. Francis de Sales

If we weren't on our way back to civilization and the registration desk
for our conference in Boise, I might have considered finding a place
to stay in Craters of the Moon. The park has been listed as an International Dark Sky Park since 2017, a designation I didn't even know
existed.

International Dark Sky Park! This could be the night—clear, cloudless,
pitch black—we could see to the ends of our atmosphere and beyond,
into the great expanse of space I've only gotten glimpses of through
someone else's camera lens. I wanted to see more before we ended the
first leg of our Wells Out West road trip—more wonder, more awe,
the kind that comes from peering up, into the "out there." Other than
the night in Clearwater Campground, I had been too tired to wait up
and slept too soundly to rise in the dead of night to check on the stars,

and anyway, I'd looked at the forecast on my phone each night, disappointed about potential cloud cover or the glow of the moon.

Maybe after Boise, when Lydia and Brandon join us and we make our way through Utah's red rocks. There's still time. As we rolled into Boise, a tumbleweed tumbled across the highway, closing a full week of being within arm's reach of my boys riding shotgun or in the back seat across the central portion of the country.

After checking into our hotel, we found a parking lot adjacent to the conference center, grabbed my box of books, and made our way toward the building.

Inside, there were people.

Even though it had only been seven days since we left Ohio, it felt like our trip had changed me. I saw the whole scene in slow motion. I pictured myself rugged and dusty, leather tan and makeup-free, walking in wearing hiking boots and a tank top, as if I'd hiked from Ohio to Idaho. Like Cheryl Strayed. As we were greeted by our friends at the conference registration table, I wondered if they noticed how I'd taken my boys through the Badlands, slept in a tent in the Shoshone National Forest, and hiked up a mountain in Yellowstone. I wondered if they saw the saunter in my steps, the way I strode into the over-air-conditioned conference center as a conqueror. *I did it. I told you I would do it, and I did it. I made it. I did this.*

There's no reason to bring up the RV, the POTS meltdown, or the luxury roadside cabin.

We grabbed our badges and youth conference T-shirts and made our way to the youth room, where dozens of kids were playing cornhole and air hockey. I found the youth leaders who would be taking care of my boys during the week while I attended the business sessions, taught a couple of breakout sessions, and manned my book table in the exhibition hall. They assured me that Elvis and Henry would be fine, we exchanged cell phone numbers, and then the strangest thing happened.

My boys left.

After a week together every hour of the day, Elvis and Henry were going away to do youth things, and me to do my adult things. Elvis left easily, but Henry and I locked eyes. The sudden ache of their departure caught me off guard.

"I guess you're off!" I said with a smile, trying to encourage both of us. "I'll be right in the exhibit hall over there. Have fun!"

As I mapped out the Plan for our Wells Out West adventure, I knew the break in Boise would be good. We would need to leave the confines of the truck for a couple of days, savor the luxury of a hotel after sleeping for *so many days on the cold, hard ground in a tent*, and be among our people for a little while. I didn't expect the lump in my throat as I watched them leave. They were eleven and nearly fifteen! It wasn't the first day of school or the first day of summer camp. It wasn't as if we would never see each other again. We were even sharing a hotel room all week! Why the sudden tears?

I shouldn't have been surprised, really. Tears well up in my chest and rise to my eyes at least once a day. The sunrise, my dogs, the way my husband gets me coffee, Elvis's smile, something Henry says, Lydia's acute emotional radar . . . you get the idea, *everything* makes me weepy.

I blame POTS, but maybe it has more to do with this particular age, this particular season. When they were little, I celebrated every passing milestone, happy that it happened, glad it was over, eager for the next season. These days, I spend so much time observing the lives unfolding in front of me. It's a powerful experience of parenting I didn't expect, this attentive awareness of life expanding and becoming more whole right before my eyes.

The infamous adolescent tension between mother and daughter has never existed between Lydia and me.

Well, that's not quite true. It lasted for about five minutes.

Lydia had just spent time with one of her best friends. This friend complained about her mother, talked down about her mother, and rolled her eyes at her mother—to her face. They had one of those infamous mother-daughter relationships that left her mother sad and bewildered, dancing around her daughter to try to find some peace.

Lydia's friend left our house, and the two of us got into the car to go to the store. I said something to Lydia. She said something mouthy and disrespectful back. Heat flared into my face and the hairs on the back of my neck stood up. What was this *attitude?!*

I looked at my daughter in the passenger seat, my mini-me, the one whose blue eyes shine like mine or like her grandmother's, depending on her mood, the girl filled with giggles and Jesus, passion and love, competitive drive and eagerness to please, who is as tall as I am now. "This is not how it's going to be between you and me," I told her, as stern as I've ever been with my strong but tender daughter. "It might be that way between other mothers and daughters, but not us. Not us."

In the movie *Spanglish,* there's a scene at the end where Flor's daughter says, "I need some space," and Flor loses it. She gets right down close to her daughter's face. "Not a space between *us!*" she said. That's how it felt.

Lydia straightened up, humbled, and said she was sorry. I immediately forgave her. In that moment in the car, it was as if we swept the floor of scattered Lego pieces of offense and cleared the way to love and respect each other, even in moments of frustration. I needed Lydia to see her small remark in light of the fullness of our relationship so she could see the implications of her words and her attitude.

And it was never like that again.

So much of my mothering these days feels like taking hold of my teenagers' shoulders to help them see beyond this moment. *Look, this is how your words can cause damage. Look, this is not so big. Look, this is where this road might head. Look, you only see right now, but I have decades of life in the rearview mirror, and I can give you a glimpse, at least, of what is yet to come, how much larger the world is, how your life is much smaller and simultaneously how you are more beloved than you can grasp.*

In January 2021, after the goodbye Zoom party my marketing colleagues threw me in which I sobbed uncontrollably, I mopped up my tears and announced to the kids that the four of us were going to Florida with my mother to celebrate the beginning of my freelance life. Brandon couldn't go, but we could slip away for a week to a cute Airbnb on Florida's gulf side. We kayaked and completed their schoolwork remotely, and I slept, a lot. Henry (9) was in love with kayaking and begged to go every chance he got. Elvis (13) moaned to turn around every five minutes, anxious about being on the water. And Lydia (14) paddled bravely and fiercely toward the horizon, leaving Henry and me in her wake. We made the most of a remote learning pandemic with my mom, who was alive and vibrant despite still having stage 4 kidney cancer. We went to Tampa's Busch Gardens, rode one of those fan boats across Florida swampland, and held an alligator, which are all things we probably wouldn't have done if my dad was there too.

I was so glad that the hard year was over and believed that once everyone was vaccinated, it would be a smooth kayak ride back to normal. After a week in the January sun, I decided that *next month*, we'd go back to Florida to hang out with the other set of grandparents. Why not? The kids are only this age once, and how many pandemics can one lifetime offer for online learning anyway?

In February, after a week at the beach with Lydia playing pickleball with her grandparents, Elvis playing video games whenever possible, and Henry insisting on swimming in the frigid Atlantic, we headed home. Halfway home, after driving all day, I ordered Outback on the app and picked it up for dinner, salivating not over steak and sweet potatoes but over the fluffy pillows and down comforter waiting for me at the hotel.

I was exhausted.

The kids turned on a movie. I slipped into pjs and prepared to eat my takeout dinner in bed when Lydia said, "Mom, I have something to tell you."

At this point, we'd spent every second of the week together and just shared 480 minutes confined in a vehicle. Surely there had been time to tell me something earlier in the day. All I wanted was to eat and close my eyes.

I took a deep breath on the precipice of *something to tell you*. I could have asked if it could wait until the morning, but if I did, would she lose confidence to approach me again later? Would she ever tell me anything again?

"What is it?"

"I'm bisexual," she said jubilantly. She practically sang it. If she was auditioning to be part of the cast of *The Prom*, she would've gotten the lead role. If there had been a Pride parade for her to enter outside the hotel that evening, she would've been the grand marshal. She was so excited—and probably relieved—to share with me the revelation of her sexuality.

I had imagined this moment: What would I do if one of our kids was gay? I pictured myself as Ideal Mother Sarah. Us crying, me embracing them, celebrating this new bit of knowledge, declaring my undying support and love, belting out "Love Thy Neighbor" alongside them in my supporting role in *The Prom*, joining them in their personal Pride parade, and being there for them *no matter what*.

"Well, good for you," I said, and ran to the bathroom.

I took some deep breaths. *Good for you?! What was I thinking?!* I wasn't thinking—I was already dreaming of sleeping. I might as well have said, "Okay, thanks for the update," as if she had said, "I like tea *and* coffee." *Well, good for you.* Just on the other side of the door, my fourteen-year-old daughter was sitting on a hotel-room double bed holding this fragile truth about herself. Her brothers were TV zombies, watching something that was too loud on a normal day but was especially too much right then. I was exhausted and lacking any mental wherewithal to give an appropriate answer to the girl who has trusted me with everything, always, ever since she could speak.

When I came out of the bathroom, I apologized and tried to start over, behaving the way Ideal Mother Sarah would have handled this moment. I would have liked to stuff this new information into the back of my long-COVID-fogged brain and never bring it up again the way the last generation of parents dealt with matters of human sexuality. I would have liked to ask a million questions, too, starting with when did you figure this out, how do you know, how long have you felt this way, are you sure, what does this mean, who else knows, why do you think this is true of yourself, what are you going to do with this newfound knowledge, how does this change everything, you know this changes everything, don't you?

Instead I asked a few questions and reserved the rest to cycle through on an endless loop in my head as I lay in bed.

Before I fell asleep, Lydia opened her arms wide and said, "I can be with anyone I want!"

I laughed and smiled at my sweet daughter. "I don't think that's quite how it works," I replied. You can't ever be with *anyone* you want, even if you're straight. There's more to it—the magnetic attraction you can't seem to resist, a necessary spark between two people, reciprocal desire that is given room to blossom, and then eventually love, committed love, faithful love, vow-bound love, love that demands boundaries and guardrails, love that must shirk the advances of anyone *else* you might want or might want you. It was cute, this naivete about what being attracted to both sexes meant to her.

After that, everyone settled into their down comforters and soft pillows and went to sleep, like their lives hadn't just changed forever.

In the month following this trip to Florida, Lydia, Brandon, and I sorted through that pile of unanswered questions together—deciding who to tell, what to say, what this meant, how short of a haircut to get, who's allowed to spend the night—and had other conversations that required asking the hardest questions. Our appreciation for the wonderfully diverse ways God has made human sexuality dominated our conversations with Lydia, but in the quiet moments between Brandon and me, we worried. How would our parents and family respond when they found out? How would our church community and friends handle this new reality? Would we continue to be accepted as church leaders?

We grieved the apparent loss of the version of our daughter's future we had always envisioned, of a traditional, nuclear family, while simultaneously hoping for her happiness and fulfillment, no matter who she ended up with. In our quietest, privatest times, we whispered, "Maybe it's a phase." Maybe this is a moment of self-exploration, and after some time, she will ultimately veer back into the sexual majority, the more known and familiar landscape we felt comfortable navigating, especially in our conservative-leaning community.

Just as we felt like we'd adjusted to the new altitude we were living in, Elvis lingered at the dinner table after the other two children left.

This one never lingers.

Brandon and I raised our eyebrows and looked at our son, waiting.

"I have something I need to tell you," he said.

I smiled encouragingly, knowing what he was going to say before he said it, because why wouldn't both of our oldest kids experience sexual identity awakenings one month apart from each other in the middle of a pandemic?

"What is it?" I asked.

Elvis sat up very straight, took a deep breath, slapped both hands against the table, and said as fast as he could, "I'm gay!"

And then he ran to his room.

It came out so fast (ha—came out—funny) that Brandon wasn't really sure what he heard. I just laughed and started to gather the plates, cleaning up from dinner, like I didn't really hear him.

"Did he say what I think he said?" Brandon asked.

"Yup," I said, rinsing off a plate.

We went to Elvis's bedroom and embraced him. This time, I said all of the things I meant to say to Lydia.

"We love you, Elvis. We will always love you. We're here for you no matter what," we said. I meant it so much that I darn near crushed him with my hug. I gave him one more squeeze and closed his door.

Brandon finished the dishes. I tidied up the dining room table. Once everything was done, we headed to the office. Closed both doors. Sat in our recliners. Turned on the TV. Texted each other "WTF is happening?!" gifs, and began researching jobs and places to move out of state, because obviously we couldn't live in Ashland or anywhere near Ashland anymore—where conservative Christian coalitions had spent the last two years winning school board elections and holding LGBTQ+ book banning rallies at the local library. The most logical, rational decision was to run far, far away from anyone and everyone who might not be able to deal with our children's sexuality. We could protect them. We could start over.

There is a space in time in each of our lives that can feel like a shattering. The hypothetical situation we entertained in the rational, untested part of our mind suddenly becomes Really Real, and now you have to decide what to do. There's what you believed about how you might respond in a particular scenario, and then there's the Scenario. What do you *do* when your child comes out to you? What do you *do* when what you believed about God's love is challenged and tested? In the blackest night, when everything else seems to be falling apart, what remains true?

In International Dark Sky territory, these three bright stars remain: faith, hope, and love. In the darkest of nights, there is no other light by which to navigate. And the greatest of these is love.

Back in the Boise conference center, Elvis and I exchanged utilitarian text messages:

MOM

GRAB MY EARBUDS PLEASE

PLEASE

MIM

MOM

TELL ME YOU HAVE YOUR PHONE

PLEASE

And later:

Hey mom

Nvm

What's up? I'm back from lunch.

Nevermind

Okay

I'm gonna drop something off at your stand

Luke bought us lunch

So . . .

I'll bring you the change too

Elvis showed up at my booth wearing a gray suit jacket and dress pants over a graphic T-shirt from *The Office*. Apparently they went thrifting, and that's how he spent most of his lunch money.

The next day, Elvis texted again, this time from a morning session:

I didn't like the session today

There were some choice words

"Billions of people, on this earth half of which are
the opposite gender you can marry"

And a few other things

I hear you there. Love you—let's talk more
buddy

Alright

Now?

I can't right now—I'm in a meeting—but afterward? Or in the car? Whichever works for you

We can talk in SLC

Mothering teens feels like dropping seeds in front of their path and dousing the ground they walk on, hoping something might take root, and then watching what happens next. I'm forever watching what happens next in a way I didn't when they were younger, when I felt some sense of power and control over whether they lived or died. I was just trying to keep them from killing themselves in one hundred small ways every day—*Don't run into the street. Don't touch the hot stove. Don't ride your bike without a helmet. Eat your vegetables.* After every single one of those phrases you could tack on "or you might die." So much of parenting little ones was keeping them from physical harm while trying to help them grow up with as few injuries, mental and physical and emotional, as possible.

With teenagers, though, I've traded my vigilance for casting visions of what once was, what could be. Here is what I learned in a similar situation. If you choose A, here are some potential scenarios. Here's how it could play out. You might want to guard your heart. You might want to turn this way instead of that. I don't know but I'm guessing that if you choose B, this is what might happen. You can choose that, but it might hurt on the other side. It might not turn out the way you hoped.

Sometime during the spring after Lydia and Elvis came out, Lydia and I took a walk. When she was younger, I began asking her if she had any questions, about anything, ask me anything, you can ask me anything! She hasn't stopped, thank God. As we walked around Ashland, we talked about her options.

"You know, being bisexual means you have some choices," I said carefully. I spent a lot of time that season trying to say so many things carefully, afraid to harm my children the way I'd seen other Christian parents injure their kids. I'm sure I've said something dumb at least a dozen times, and I'll probably say many more dumb things before I'm through too.

"Being attracted to both sexes means that, in some ways, you have a decision to make about the kind of future you want to have. And each of your choices are going to have consequences. Let's say you fall in love with another woman and decide to get married. Knowing what we both know about our small town—and other small towns like it—that could impact where you feel safe living. It could impact the places you feel safe worshipping. It'll change the way you have a family. No matter which way you decide to go, it *will* be good, but it will also be *different*. There will be challenges no matter which way you take. You *could* stay in a small town, but it's probably going to be harder."

As we walked, I told her how I'd been attracted to lots of different people in my life, and that attraction is only one part of the marriage equation. I told her that she might be bisexual but she's also so much more than her sexuality, she's also my daughter, a friend, a grand-daughter, a beloved child of God, and all of these facets of her identity matter, too. I encouraged her to pray—not to pray the gay away, but to pray for the Lord's guidance in her life, so that she might be able to discern how he made her and who he made her and what steps she should take to lead the most whole, abundant, and free life in Christ.

In short, we talked a lot.

What I've realized in this season is that my teens are adults-in-training. Now is the time to begin awakening them to the expansiveness of their world. They will always be, in some ways, the center of their personal universes. We're all the main characters of our lives, but in order to operate with any kind of grace and love, sometimes we have to surrender the first-person point of view and see. *Look.*

It's time to practice adulting. It's time to test their own paths. Now is a great time for it, too, because I still have two or three or seven years with them, depending on which kid we are talking about, and I'm a close distance to catch them when they make mistakes, to guide them where they'll let me, and to pour as much love and reassurance into them about the truth they still can't really see, the truth that they bear the image of God.

But mostly in this season, I get to ask questions, and love, and watch.

So I watched my kids start to date, and as they dated, I asked questions. I watched my kids select different hairstyles and dye what was left of it pink and purple and blue and then decide that really wasn't for them and grow it out again. I watched them choose different clothing and buy rainbow everything, and I cautioned them to, you know, maybe keep their sexuality a little close in this season, maybe give it a minute, maybe avoid slapping rainbow everything into every social media post, at least until the dust settled a little. I watched them try to date their friends despite my advice not to. Sure, friends can become soulmates, but I had tried to date a friend in high school, too, and it had ruined our friendship.

Mom, you were right, that was a mistake.

Not that I'm always right . . . but I am quite often right.

I listened to Elvis worry about our non-affirming denomination and saw his heart for the rest of his misfit friends. *I love many things about being Brethren,* I tell him, *many things. But this is one thing I don't agree with.* Even as I serve and love within the context of our denomination, I worry that the church at large has made sexuality an issue of salvation, effectively slamming the door on people who simply have questions about who they are and how God made them. I want the broken and beautiful body of believers to be a safe place, for love to cover over all. I want the church to make room for the long road, the same way God has been patient with me, the same way God has been patient with all of us, not wanting any to perish, but all to come to repentance.[10] Instead of posting No Trespassing signs, I hope the church will give my children space to discover who they are in Christ and to let Christ reign in their hearts, to let the Holy Spirit call them into the life God has for them. Isn't that what we all want for our children, for God's children?

My son's friends have taken different first names and showed up at my house looking dejected and alone only to open up and smile a few weeks later, within the safety and security of our home. My freelance job gives me the liberty to be there when the kids come home, to know their friends' names, to greet them when the dogs announce their arrival, to feed them, and to love them when so many in our community have chosen to call them unlovable. I observe it all and hope against hope they absorb some of this love, my love.

---

10 2 Peter 3:9.

The New York Times columnist David Brooks reminded me of a word recently that captures this kind of watching: *beholding*. I have the distinct pleasure to behold their beloved-ness, behold the image of God in them. No one could have cued me into this privilege, to witness the becoming of my children and their friends. I like "behold." The past tense of it could be "beheld," to be beholden by someone is to be held.

These days, I feel like my teens need to be held loosely. Sometimes what I want to do is cling tighter. What I want to do is direct their paths and protect them from all harm, like their lives are on rails and I'm the railroad engineer. What I think they need from me are guardrails and GPS, and let me tell you, I know how to make a Plan.

Instead God whispers, *Hold on loosely*. They need clear guidance, yes, but I need the heartbreaking understanding that they might choose to turn left when I thought they should turn right. They need grace to make the decisions, and grace when they turn around. Isn't that what the Generous and Extravagant Father does for the Prodigal Son? He lets him go with open arms and he welcomes him back, running like a fool to embrace him when he returns.

Watching them come into their own is a special kind of wonder and delight. It's such a privilege to watch the people you brought into the world become more wholly themselves, to watch them try on different identities, to see them seek out new hobbies and passions, to observe the way they light up when they've hit upon that Thing, the Thing that makes their hearts sing and their neurons fire, the "deep gladness" Frederick Buechner says will help them find their vocation, there at the intersection of the world's deep need. And I get to be here, all weepy and gushy and cheesy, watching it unfurl.

When my kids were younger and I was working full-time at the university, my friend Jody told me she thought her kids were needy when they were little, but the time they *really* needed her was in junior high and high school. Just as she'd head to bed, someone would softly knock on the door and ask, "Mom?" and then the night would begin. That seemed to be true for mine, too, especially in the last few years. Resigning from Spire aligned with the beginnings of a wild roller-coaster ride with our oldest two. I don't know how I would have navigated this season if I had also still been trying to work and recover from COVID.

Even with the challenges of adolescence, my life has been so much slower since I began freelancing. There's so much more time to notice what's happening right in front of me instead of rushing through today in anticipation of what might happen tomorrow. That expanse of time and space has allowed me to be still enough to notice my children. It has left room for them to linger around the dining room table. It has carved opportunities for us to knock on a closed door and ask, "You seem off. Is everything okay?" Slowing down made room for us to notice things we might have missed before the Great Emergency Brake of 2020.

This paired with intense awareness of the rapid passing away of all things seems to keep me in a constant state of wonder, which ultimately spills over in the form of tears, happy sighs, and a gushy, joyful proclamation, "I love sunsets."

"*I love sunsets,*" my children echo mockingly, lovingly, which only makes me grin and weep some more. Mock away! I think to myself. Let me draw your attention to the lovely, true, and beautiful, even if you think I'm a total cheeseball.

Which I am, and you *love* it.

Nine months after my dad learned about Lydia, she knocked on our bedroom door and asked if she could come in.

Lydia had spent a lot of time exploring what it meant for her to be bisexual. Her sexuality had evolved from the focal point of her identity to just one part of who she is.

"I want the traditional family, the husband and kids, and when I picture my future, that's what I see," she said. "Even if I am attracted to both sexes."

She lamented that the rainbow stickers and Pride parades were for nothing, because she arrived in the same place she started. She felt like she could have avoided a lot of tension and struggle.

I wrapped my arms around her. "Oh, honey, it wasn't for nothing. You asked important questions about yourself and you found answers."

Self-discovery is a lifelong journey, an invitation from the Lord to lean in and learn more about the desires of our heart. Nothing is wasted. These journeys of self-discovery are always fruitful because they lead us to truth. They lead us home.

Most of the time on our road trip Elvis spent texting with Finch, his first serious partner. It was the beginning of a long, complicated, on-again, off-again relationship that would ultimately do more harm than good for both of them. Over the next two years, Brandon and I struggled to decide how much to intervene, how much to hold on, how much to restrict, and how much to just watch. It took Elvis a full year to recover and heal from the damage, but he did. He did.

On our WOW trip, though, the road was still new and he was making his way, too, trying to figure out who he is and how God made him and where he will walk in this world. And I am so glad I am here for it.

For the last week, I'd been gawking with Elvis and Henry at sources of wonder and awe, pointing, "Look!" and shouting, "Wow!" This week in Boise felt like a foretaste of things to come: my boys galloping away, not forever, just for now, until someday in the future when they will pack themselves up and trot right out the door.

As I walked toward the exhibit hall at the end of our week, Elvis bounded toward me in his thrift-store suit and a grin, with Henry following beside him. There they were, my children, my precious, quirky, undeniably loved and adored and made-in-the-image-of-God children. *May the door of the church never swing shut on their beautiful souls,* I thought to myself as Elvis swung his lanky arms around me and squeezed.

"You guys ready to go?" I asked. "Time to get on the road—Salt Lake City, here we come!"

Why Lot's Wife Turned to Look Back

Antelope Island State Park, Salt Lake City, Utah

I'm told this is where the deer and the antelope play
with free-ranging bison and bighorn sheep,
where we can take a dip in the lake's salty water
and stroll along sandy beaches our parents walked, once.
They said it was glorious—it took no faith at all to float.

From the parking lot, the lake shimmers. It doesn't look
so far to reach the receding hairline of the Great Salt Lake,
so I take off my shoes like Moses to feel the shore on my feet.
We walk and walk. Sand turns to crystallized seabed salt
and rock. It's just a little farther, almost within reach.

I only want to say that the water rippled over our toes as the sun
began to set—every hope I had was realized, I floated,
Utah's population of wildlife resurrected itself and sang—
but we stand on dry ground where water used to be. When
Lot's wife turned, it was only in sorrow. Everywhere I look,

there's salt. The pads of my feet are tender, the shoreline no line,
just a murky mud puddle. We turn and walk the long path back,
no buffalo, no antelope, no shrimp or boats in sight. Go ahead,
turn and look back, look at how the sun burns the mountain ridge,
look how it reflects off the diamonds we thought we might have

to walk on forever, watch the mirage in this evaporating terrain.

Chapter 8

Waist-Deep in Zion

We picked up the rest of the Wells family from the Salt Lake City airport on Friday after spending all day Thursday driving from Boise. I had booked an Airbnb on the south side of Salt Lake City for two nights—to recuperate from the conference and catch up on laundry, to reunite our family after eleven days apart, and to explore some of Salt Lake City, especially the Great Salt Lake itself. From Salt Lake City, the Plan was to head to the far end of Utah to see Zion, Bryce, and Arches. Salt Lake City marked the beginning of our spare-no-expense-within-reason leg of the Wells Out West trip, which meant we'd stay in actual *hotels* and eat out. There would be none of that "roughin' it" business—no PB&J sandwiches, no rest stop lunches, no pretend-sleeping in tents. My husband and daughter weren't cut out for all of that.

Outside, at the arrivals area, Brandon and Lydia walked toward us with the same degree of determination and stride, both carrying a single backpack. They had packed some clothes for us to take with us in the truck so they didn't have to check any bags.

"It's so good to see you!" I cheered, getting out to hug my people. I nestled into Brandon's embrace, inhaled the aroma of my husband, and felt all of the tension drain out of me. *Ah, home,* I breathed. The two of them swung their stuff into the bed of the truck and climbed in. I surrendered the driver's seat to Brandon, and Lydia climbed into the back with the boys.

There's nothing like the five of us together, I thought with a grin, relaxing into the passenger seat. Our family unit understands each other's sense of humor. We think the same thoughts. We say the same things simultaneously, as if we're sharing the same huge Wells brain.

The five of us headed out together to explore Salt Lake City, visit Antelope Island, and then make our way south through Utah to Zion.

I first visited Zion National Park with my parents on our out west trip the summer I turned sixteen. I had just started dating my friend Mike that summer, convinced that we'd get married when I graduated high school in two years. I was super ready to get out of the back seat of that minivan and move on with my life. I journaled throughout the trip in letter form, writing to "My Michael" about the front porch and pet cocker spaniel we'd have, dreaming about a future I thought I wanted and relentlessly annoyed about how much driving we were doing.

After hours and hours of driving, Zion was the first park I felt like we truly *experienced.* Even though we did the dam tour at the Hoover Dam and stopped to walk a little bit into Sequoia to see the big trees, to me, no visit in a park ever felt like enough. I always longed to stay longer, to linger in nature, to be in a space instead of just seeing the space. It felt like the minute we put our feet on the ground, my dad was urging us to turn around and get back into the minivan. I would sigh dramatically and trudge away from whatever waterfall, pine-strewn path, or rock formation waited for me just ahead on the trail. I was never satisfied.

From my sixteen-year-old back seat vantage point, it felt like all we did on that trip was drive.

Of *course* all we did was drive—when your father is on a mission to give you the out west trip of *his* childhood and show you all those same parks in just ten days, that's what you have to do. You have to drive and drive and drive. All we've done is drive for the vast majority of *our* out west trip. There is no other way.

But that all changed in Zion. We got out of the car in Zion. We walked a *trail* in Zion. We literally waded in water in Zion!

I wonder now if my irritable, hormonal whining and Dramamine-induced rage influenced the way my mom and dad navigated the last leg of our out west trip together. (In the Wells household, we call it DramaMEAN, because Mom wakes up from her drug-induced nap ready to murder everyone if there isn't a plan to stop for Chick-fil-A immediately.) At sixteen, I did not hide my frustration and disappointment. It didn't occur to me until just now, decades later, that maybe, in the same way I am hyper-attuned to my children's moods and wishes, my parents picked up on the vibes I was throwing down. Maybe they made space for their never-enough, always-disappointed daughter and tried to satisfy that hunger.

From our hike in Zion, I remember tall canyon walls of bright red rock and a gentle, steady current. I hold in my head a still photo of my brothers, shirtless in blue jean shorts, framed by red canyon walls, holding walking sticks and grinning. I remember my mother being delighted about the canyon, her children, the water, and life, and my father being anxious about the boys going too far or slipping or breaking a bone or drowning in the shin-deep stream. But perhaps most of all, I remember a gnawing longing of being so far up the river and wanting to go farther. It was definitely more exploring than the first leg of the trip, but when Dad made the call to turn around on The Narrows trail, I hesitated and stared toward the bend in the river, aching for *more*. It still wasn't enough for me.

Sitting in the passenger seat next to Brandon, I wanted to give all of it to our kids—the river hike, the canyon, the overwhelming awe, *and* the gnawing longing for more, more, and even more, more awe around the next bend, more awe around this corner.

Maybe as the one in charge of this trip, I could give them enough, and they would be satisfied.

Before we could get to the awe, we drove past some yellow flashing signs. I had seen the signs leading into Zion that said "Zion Parking Full; Take Shuttle from Springside," but we arrived later in the day. *Surely people had left the park already and freed up space inside,* I thought to myself and said to no one.

We drove past Springside and past the barricaded turn for The Narrows, up switchback after switchback, up and up and up, with nary a parking spot in sight. Cars seemed to dangle off the side of red cliffs, rubber tires and parking brakes breathlessly clinging to the sandstone underneath them. We drove on, farther and farther from The Narrows turnoff, up to, into, and through the mile-long tunnel that weaves in and out of the side of the canyon wall. On the other side of the tunnel, we turned around so we could try again with the whole parking thing.

"Ah! There's one!" I shouted, pointing to an empty space on the other side of the road. Brandon kept driving, looking for an opportunity to turn around. Meanwhile, other cars steered toward the one vacant parking spot in all of Utah. I started sweating a little. This is how we would spend our time in Zion. The sun would set and the canyon would cool and we'd still be driving back and forth through the switchbacks, looking for a vacant space.

It took us forty-five minutes, but finally we found a spot our truck could fit in. Brandon turned on his blinker and started parallel parking along the cliff edge. Four backseat drivers groaned and recoiled from the right-hand side of the car as if leaning toward the left was the maneuver that would keep the truck from skidding down into the ravine.

We all teetered out, careful not to die.

Victory was ours! At last, we could make our way to The Narrows. I breathed a sigh of relief and gave my husband a reassuring smile. *We did it,* I said with my eyes, *we have overcome the Zion National Park Parking Space Crisis. We can do anything!*

We crossed the road at the next opening in traffic and hiked up to shuttle stop 3. The five of us wiped the sweat from our foreheads, sat down on the benches, and waited. Henry slurped water through the CamelBak straw. Elvis pulled out his phone. No one else was at shuttle stop 3. Some folks walked by from farther up the road. They did not stop at shuttle stop 3. I stood up and walked over to read the map on the wall of the overhang.

"Oh," I said. Based on the information on the wall, I considered what to say and how to say it to try to manage the emotions of my small tribe of hikers.

This is the history of Sarah summed up in one sentence: What can I do to try to manage the expectations of other people so I don't disappoint them?

It is my greatest fear and deepest need, to avoid letting people down. I want to *matter* to people. If I fall short of someone's unspoken expectations, it feels devastating. Striving to be perfect and taking pride in my performance as a human is the dandelion that probably took root in our family's motto, *Fugmans are hard workers*, and went to seed in me in high school. By the time I hit college, those seeds had spread and taken over the whole flower bed. I wanted to be perfect, and if I fell short, I would be letting everyone down.

For that reason, grace has not come easily to me.

Unearned favor? Love just because? How irrational! How illogical! How unjust! You've got to *earn* approval, and to *earn* it, you need to be perfect. Who needs forgiveness when you can just feel absolutely mortified by your own personal failures, no matter how few and far between you imagine them being?

For this reason, I have something of a reputation back in Ashland. Those of us who attended 5 Stones Community Church in 2013 remember fondly our summer At the Movies series in which our pastor guided us through a different movie each week, drawing out the gospel embedded in those stories. I ran slides at church back then. I am an accomplished slide runner, the *best* at queuing up song lyrics for the congregation at *just the right time*, anticipating the next line and advancing the slide *just so*. Simply the best.

This particular Sunday the film was *Jerry Maguire*. We'd rehearsed the timing for the five different clips twice that morning to make sure that Cuba Gooding Jr. would not once and not ever begin to say "No heart?! No heart! I'm all heart . . ." We all know what he says next, but that does not mean it ought to be said. On Sunday. In church. During a sermon.

The sermon began, and I shared the first couple clips. As the clock ticked closer to the queued-up cutoff point, I thought to myself, *Oh no. What if the DVD doesn't stop at the forty-second mark?* ProPresenter makes this process simple. Foolproof, even. All you do is set the time it's supposed to begin and set the time it's supposed to end. The machine does the rest. Done.

But.

What if this time *the DVD keeps playing?* I thought. The church was filled with new college students back from summer break and new families visiting for the first time. *What if the DVD keeps playing and the whole church watches the end of this scene?*

So I positioned the mouse arrow over the play/pause button and prepared myself to stop the DVD *just in case* we hit the forty-second mark and it kept playing. We hit the forty-second mark. I panicked. I clicked the play/pause button just as the clip paused like it was supposed to. *It kept playing.* "No heart?!" Cuba Gooding Jr. said. OH NO.

"No heart?!" Cuba Gooding Jr. said, "I'm ALL HEART, m*f*!"

EEEEEEEEEEEEKK! I shrieked, frantically clicking the play/pause button, the stop button, any button to make it stop, make it stop, JUST MAKE IT STOP! And then it was over, the church collectively gasping and laughing, the pastor laughing and apologizing and asking for forgiveness and the congregation granting it, because we were a merciful, grace-filled congregation. From the balcony behind my computer screen I yelled down, *I am so sorry.*

Mortified. Failure. Huge disappointment.

My entire body reacted throughout the rest of the sermon, hands trembling, adrenaline pumping, head shaking, tear ducts leaking impulsively. *OMG. That just happened. OMG.* I made it through the rest of the morning, and despite my horror, the congregation received me with grace and laughter.

It was very difficult for me to receive grace. I wanted the A. I wanted more than good, more than good enough, more than great: I wanted perfect. I *expected* perfection from myself. Not from others, no, I understood that others aren't perfect and that everyone messes up and blah blah blah, yes, other people, but *not me.*

When I fail, I expect condemnation. Disappointment. Rejection. Instead, I was met with laughter and grace. Christ is all about grace, and I suspect he also laughs.

But still. "No heart?! I'm all heart!"

God, help me. From now on, you can call me Sarah "All Heart" Wells.

Having read the writing on the wall, I prepared myself to deliver the bad news to my family.

"Shuttle stop 3 is an outbound shuttle stop only. I think that means we can't go up to The Narrows from here," I said, and waited for the slouching and groaning.

"You serious, Clark?" Brandon said, quoting *Christmas Vacation.* I laughed, relieved. So far, despite the lack of parking spaces and the closed routes and the shuttle bus reconfiguration, all of which felt to me like personal failures, the five of us had managed to keep clinging to the life raft of hope that The Narrows was going to be *awesome,* no matter what detours we faced.

With less enthusiasm and more weariness, we said, *No worries, it's the federal government, of course it's this cumbersome.* We caught the next southbound shuttle to the visitor center, disembarked, and reboarded a bus to the Temple of Sinawava. The Temple and The Narrows are the most popular parts of Zion, and despite arriving at The Narrows nearly two hours later than when we first entered the park, there were loads of people with us, eager to enter the Virgin River.

We reached the Temple of Sinawava. Around us, walls of hanging gardens and red rock jutted over three thousand feet toward heaven. The sun cascaded off the sandstone as we walked with our fellow travelers. We dripped sweat. Dust caked my shins.

I knew, once my feet hit the cool flow of the Virgin River, that all would be well. Just a little farther, just a little farther, and we would be waste-deep in Zion. We hiked the paved Riverside Trail one mile to the trailhead for The Narrows until the pavement ended.

"This is it!" I said with glee. Standing on the precipice of the river felt like that moment before you stepped onto the automated people mover at an airport, that moment before you launched from one way of moving in the world to another: accelerated and exhilarating. The water flowed uninterrupted around our legs, impartial to our moods and delays.

I felt so proud. My people were keeping it together! Despite what felt like a thousand mishaps and possible disappointments, no one had gotten crispy with each other. I beamed at each of my people as if to say, "See? Look around you! Isn't this marvelous? Isn't it wonderful? Wasn't all that failure worth it?"

The Virgin River had taken the last 18 million years to carve this awesome slot canyon, running sixteen miles long and over two thousand feet deep. It took us several hours of patience and perseverance powered by the Holy Spirit to finally arrive here.

I'm not sure which was more impressive.

I have spent so much of my life afraid of disappointing people— basically everyone—but underneath that fear is a greater fear. Maybe I am not enough. If I do not live up to your expectations, then I am not worthy of your love. If I let you down, you will reject me.

No heart? I shout out with Cuba Gooding Jr. Am I not enough for you? Am I too much for you? *No heart?* Let me prove myself to you! You'll see! *I'm all heart!*

But at various points in the last few years, in the quietest, tenderest, most gentle of ways, God has insisted, *You are my daughter, whom I love. In you, I am well pleased. I am not disappointed in you. You are my beloved, no matter what.*

It will take me an entire lifetime of daily submission and obedience to the voice of the Lord to actually believe those words.

"The last time I did this, I was courting your mother," Brandon told the kids as we hiked.

It was what I did with boyfriends, I guess, because I'd invited other guys before him to go river walking with me. It must have been a subconscious test of their loyalty—could they rough it with me? Did they love the outdoors as much as I did, or enough to cut it? There was something romantic and intimate to me about balancing precariously on wet boulders and being in the flow of waterfalls. Rivers are places of peace and God's presence for me. When I am hot and irritable, annoyed or impatient, lonely or disappointed, I can always count on water to bring me back to center. I have gravitated to water for this holy settling in my spirit even before I knew how to name it.

We had been dating for just a week or so when I told Brandon we should go river walking in the Chagrin River in the Cleveland Metroparks. He had never done such a thing, growing up in the city, but he didn't tell me, of course. He teetered from rock to dry rock while I maneuvered across the slippery bottom, eager to get to the waterfall. At one point, he stepped on the sharp end of a pair of broken sunglasses and cut the bottom of his foot. He didn't tell me about that, either, and kept on going, following me through the river.

I could not understand why this was not Brandon's idea of a good time. All I was thinking about was how romantic this moment was, how perfect we were for each other, how clear it was that we would be together forever. All his anxiety-fueled mind was probably thinking about was how he'd need to have his foot amputated in a few months after a prolonged infection that would likely begin that day in the river, thanks to those broken sunglasses and his choice of Birkenstocks for creek walking. Who was this chick, and what had she gotten him into?!

Somehow, Brandon asked me on another date after that. Or maybe I did the asking? It's all kind of a blur to me.

That was over twenty years ago. Now, here he was, willingly soaked so that the five of us could be a part of building the same life-long memory.

Talk about loyalty. Like that day in the Chagrin River, Brandon let me lead the way through The Narrows, walking along with our two oldest children as Henry bounded back and forth, ahead and behind. Lydia was on edge, unsure if she loved or hated this experience. Elvis seemed to be having fun but also disliked wearing wet clothes. Henry was drenched from head to toe. He caught a current along the edge of the river and rode it like a waterslide, crossing his arms across his chest and leaning back flat against the water.

I waded in joy. I wept with gratitude. With one eye on the canyon ahead, I kept turning around to make sure each of my people were having the best time ever.

When I stepped down from my job and stepped into my slow and steady recovery, Brandon and I continued to take walks each day when he returned home from work.

"How was your day?" I'd ask, and he'd tell me.

"How about you, how was your day?" he'd ask.

"Great! I wrote an article today!" I might say, or "I wrote some social posts for a client," or "I did the laundry."

"You know," Brandon said more than once, "you could stay in bed all day. You could read a book all day. You don't have to justify your existence to me."

But what if I'm not enough? What if it's not enough to just be me?

The Israelites in the Bible had a practice for marking monumental events in their history. When they crossed the Jordan River on dry ground into the Promised Land, the Levites collected Stones of Remembrance—twelve large stones from the Jordan riverbed, gathered together on the shore. Joshua told the people, "In the future, when your children ask you, 'What do these stones mean?' tell them . . ."

Tell them what happened here. Tell them their history; share with them their legacy. Help them understand where they came from, how that shaped you, and who they are as a result.

It is said that you never step into the same river twice. As I wade through the Virgin River and turn each stone of remembrance over, I can see the memories changing right in front of me, shifting perspective and reshaping me.

In my memory of that first hike through The Narrows, I see myself sandwiched between my parents and my brothers. The two boys—so much younger than me at eight and twelve—held onto their sticks and hiked in wet jean shorts through the rippling, red canyon stream. Until now I had no vision of where my parents stood in that river, no idea what it was like to be thirty-six and forty, to watch how far your children had come and imagine where they were going. I just knew where I had been and where I wanted to be.

Now I imagine them trailing behind us, vigilant, trying to make a way for us, waiting for someone to slip, waiting for something to happen, waiting for the right moment to call us back and out of the waters. Hoping that maybe, this time, Sarah would be satisfied, Sarah would not be disappointed.

After a half hour of walking upstream, we came to the place where the river bends. This, I thought to myself, is the place our family turned around when I was a kid, the place I so longed to press further into, to keep going and going and going, hiking all sixteen miles, finding the narrowest parts of the canyon, wading while the sun set and setting up camp like *real* hikers.

I knew there was more ahead to explore. I looked at Henry. He was soaked, head to toe, wading in the deepest waters of the river, hiking in one of the grandest canyons on Earth. Would he be disappointed if we turned around right now? How much farther would it take to satisfy either of our adventurer's hearts? If we kept going, would we discover a passage of The Narrows that would mark this trip as a success, that would leave us stunned and in even greater awe, in even greater wonder?

As Henry charged ahead, I turned to the rest of my family. Were they satisfied, even if I was not? Lydia looped her thumbs under her backpack straps and gave me her best sticking-with-it grin. Elvis looked at me with soft eyes and a smile, hands on his hips. Brandon waited, raising an eyebrow and nodding toward the bend in the river, the unspoken question of whether we would keep going on his lips.

Awe and wonder weren't tucked around the next bend. They were right there.

"We should probably turn around," I told Brandon. My husband knows my longing for more and my desire to see and experience this world, and he knows the depths of my disappointment when I feel like someone is trying to cut the moment short, before I've been able to fully experience the edge of something beautiful. He *knows* me, so instead of following his own desire to get back onto dry ground, he waited for me to be satisfied. He let me say when it was enough.

"Thank GOD!" Lydia shouted. Elvis and Brandon were quick to pivot, too.

Henry looked upstream, toward the bend in the river.

"Henry boy," I said, "time to head back." He turned reluctantly but quickly recovered, finding his way into the deepest carved chutes of sandstone in the river to be caught up in the current once more.

As solid as rock might be, the water keeps flowing, the sandstone eroding. I gazed one final time at the bend in the rocks, slowly changed by water over 18,000 millenia, and turned to hike out of The Narrows with my family just a few feet in front of me.

Sonnet Math

The Narrows, Zion National Park

When I was here last I was sixteen,
my parents were thirty-six and forty;
now, I hover on the red cliff of forty,
amazed to be the mother of a sixteen-

year-old. I'm caught up in this stream
of thought as the river rolls relentless,
keep calling our sons by my brothers'
names. At some point we will need

to double back. How much farther
can we travel 'til we make the turn?
Maybe then we'll know the way, turn
and trace our erased steps, carve our

place in canyon walls that laugh
as we attempt to master sonnet math.

Chapter 9

The Hoodoo That You Do

*I believe people might amaze themselves with their ingenuity,
energy, creativity, and modesty if their modus operandi became
a deep conviction that God laughs and plays.*

—David James Duncan, *God Laughs and Plays*

I have a vivid childhood memory of a picture of a brown-haired Jesus laughing heartily, his head thrown back and luscious locks shimmering angelic in the back lighting.

I don't know exactly what he was laughing at, but that image is mashed in my head with the saying, "When man plans, God laughs."

That's right, the beautiful Son of God portrait is laughing at us in mockery. A plan?! You want to *plan*?! This is especially annoying for someone who *loves* to plan.

The Plan for our trip out of Zion National Park and onward toward Bryce Canyon was to arrive at our lodging around seven o'clock to grab a bite to eat at a restaurant.

Once back in the truck, I told Brandon, "Okay, turn around and head back toward the entrance." I couldn't get cell service but felt fairly certain that there was only one way out of Zion, back the way we came. You know, like a zoo.

As we neared the entrance, I visualized in my head the Google Map route I'd made. Something felt wrong.

"Wait. I think our place is back the other way," I said. "I'm sorry."

Brandon sighed, laughed, and turned around again. We made our way back to the switchbacks, up and up and up, through the tunnel, calling out, "Look, kids, Big Ben!" (I guess Chevy Chase films really made an impression on us).

Because of the concentrated number of people in the main area of the park, I thought that Zion was small, just this one amazing trail through an ancient canyon carved from a pristine river. In my memory, that's how I had experienced Zion as a teenager. The truth, of course, is that Zion is huge. At nearly 150,000 acres, it isn't the largest of national parks, but it's still roughly the same size as Chicago.

Once we got our GPS back, I realized just how far we were from Pinewoods Resort, the place we planned to stay that night. We had miles and miles of red canyon walls to go.

We finally arrived at Pinewoods Resort in time to eat dinner before the Pinewoods Grille closed at nine. I had hoped to be there earlier to take advantage of the amenities on their website—a pool, a hot tub, a game room, and a firepit. I had envisioned us sitting around together, eating s'mores underneath a clear night sky, admiring the Milky Way perfectly positioned in the open view between a forest of tall, dark ponderosa pines. Pinewoods Resort promised the perfect end to our Narrows adventure.

But by the time we were done eating, we were also done doing anything else except sleeping.

"Well, the Plan was to get up early and catch the sunrise over Bryce Canyon tomorrow," I told my slouching, sleepy family sitting across from one another in a red vinyl booth. "But maybe we should just . . . sleep. What do you think?"

No one protested. We paid our bill, bypassed the firepit, and headed out of the restaurant. The kids stopped briefly to check out the pool but returned quickly. We all turned on the fans in our rooms and crawled into the beds in the rustic condo. It wasn't what I had expected, but it was a place to sleep, and Bryce Canyon was just a quick hour away in the morning.

Somewhere in the hidden constellations that night, a laughing Jesus head mocked all my plans.

Back in Boise at our church conference, I joined Dr. Steven Cole, then executive director/pope of the Brethren national office, for lunch. We grabbed some food and sat down to discuss what waited for me back in Ashland when our trip was over.

"So, tell me about the new job! Where did *that* come from?" Steven asked.

I chuckled. "Well, Brandon is going back to finish seminary this fall," I said between bites of my salad. "But he's also planning on quitting his job when we return from vacation. He hasn't said anything yet, obviously, but that's the plan. We've been talking about what the future looks like for him, and his current position isn't sustainable. When the possibility of him quitting came up, we started to play out various scenarios, financially, to see how we could make it work."

Steven ate his sandwich while I kept talking, my fork full of romaine and cheese hovering above my salad. "On a whim, I thought I'd check to see if there was anything open at the university. The website had a listing for a part-time position supporting the honors program. After I inquired and realized that the position wouldn't meet our needs, the interim dean stepped in and asked whether I'd be interested in full-time. I wasn't, but for the right amount of money and a four-day workweek most of the year, it might work. So," I sighed, taking a break and eating a bite, "they combined the part-time position with supporting two master's programs, including the Master of Fine Arts in Creative Writing—which, as you know, I'm well acquainted with."

I was suddenly very tired from all of this explaining. Steven was basically done eating, and I'd taken only a couple of bites. I took another forkful before continuing. "They gave me the contract I asked for, there's insurance, my kids will have free tuition if they decide to go to college, and the job gives Brandon the permission he needed to take the leap into seminary full-time."

"Wow," Steven replied. "I thought you really enjoyed freelancing."

"I *love* freelancing," I acknowledged, brightening at the memory of my beautiful life as a freelancer. "It's the gig I never thought I'd have and never dreamed to ask for, and it was just the right thing for me the last year and a half as I recovered from COVID. God has been *so good to me*. But," I said, taking a deep breath and another stab at that salad, "it's time for me to put my big girl pants back on."

Brandon had given me room so many times in the last nineteen years to pursue my career at the expense of his own. Every move we made as a family has been because of *my* career, *my* job change, *my* dreams. If sacrificing my freelance gig for another job would allow him to run after the calling he felt, then that's what I'd do.

Plus, there were only a couple more years until our kids would be safely beyond the tumultuous junior and senior high years. No more late-night knocks on my bedroom door. No more identity questions or college searches or football concession stands to man. What would I do then? Did it really make sense for me to continue freelancing after they graduated? Shouldn't I get back to the *real world*, where people work forty hours or more a week, tolerate their jobs, and complain about being exhausted?

Steven nodded. "I had looked forward to working with you on some projects this fall, but it doesn't sound like you're going to have time for those now," he said.

I had forgotten about the work we'd discussed doing. "Oh, well," I said, feeling disappointed and guilty, "I *did* ask for a flexible workweek, which will allow me to keep doing some writing jobs. It's the only way I could justify the salary cut, and writing is such an important part of my life. I'm sure I can make time for your projects with that extra day off each week."

The reality of this shift suddenly made my heart ache. It all happened so quickly. I had hardly processed the decision to take on this new position with anyone except my mom and Brandon, and even then, I had approached the job opportunity biased. This was my chance to Save the MFA Program. It was meant to be. I could be Super Sarah and return to the university where I had so many allies and friends. Our children could be free from college debt, all because of me. I would come home to my alma mater, again, and probably stay until I retired.

It seemed so obvious at the time that *this* was the Plan. This was the Purpose. But was it, really?

"If God is not juice and joy, then who has created all these lilacs and lilies?"

—Richard Rohr, *Adam's Return*

Setting aside the idea of a mocking God, I love the idea of God laughing. It isn't the image most people conjure when they think about the Lord of the universe. If asked, "Old Man with a Beard and Robe" would probably top the *Family Feud* list of images of God. Survey says...! Maybe next in line would be the judgy, cranky God in the clouds from *Monty Python and the Holy Grail*, or Michaelangelo's God, aloof in the clouds of the Sistine Chapel. Perhaps Aslan, the lion from The Chronicles of Narnia, would make the list, a God of strength and royalty, sacrifice and bravery, gentleness and, yes, just a little playfulness. Or the all-time most-reproduced image of Jesus, Warner Sallman's light-eyed, light-haired, placid-looking "Head of Christ."

To me, that "Jesus Laughing" pencil sketch by Ralph Kozak from 1977 is the most compelling illustration of the God I love to follow. I want to sit around a campfire telling stories and rehashing my dad's favorite old joke about the guy with the wooden eye to make Jesus laugh like that. A laughing Jesus embodies the fruit of the Spirit, which is first love, then joy, then a whole bunch of other fruit we'd munch on together as we reminisced about the good ol' days. When you think of a face filled with love and joy, isn't it one tipped back to the sky with crinkly eyes and a wide grin?

I am drawn to and admire the images we have of the suffering servant, too, whose suffering breaks my heart and makes me weep for the injustice of it all, whose suffering, death, and ultimate resurrection gives me hope for all of life's greatest trials and pain. But couldn't we all use just a few more laughing Jesuses, images that seem to represent the abundant life into which we've been invited by that very Son of Man? Maybe more like Santa?

And why not like Santa? Bearer of undeserved gifts, beacon of joy and generosity, St. Nicholas of peace and kindness, whose belly shook when he laughed like a bowl full of jelly, that patron saint of sailors, merchants, archers, repentant thieves, prostitutes, children, brewers, pawnbrokers, unmarried people, and students in various cities and countries around Europe (according to Wikipedia) . . . isn't our Lord even better than he?

David James Duncan's book *God Laughs and Plays* is worth the purchase for the title alone, which comes from a Meister Eckhart quote, "Truly! Truly! By God! By God! Be as sure of it as you are that God lives: at the least good deed done here in this world, the least bit of good will, the least good desire, all the saints in heaven and on earth rejoice, and together with the angels their joy is such that all the joy in this world can't be compared. But the joy of them all together amounts to as little as a bean when compared to the joy of God over good deeds. For truly, God laughs and plays."

God laughs and plays, and nowhere is it more on display than in Utah's wilderness playgrounds. He's been busy playing since the dawn of creation, unfolding galaxies and stars, solar systems and planets, moons and one elegantly positioned blue-green marble that is perfectly suited for all of this abundance to explode every season over millions of years. Maybe I'm biased since I don't have any lived experience on any other planets, but I think God must love Earth especially. Look what fun things have been given space to evolve here!

In Arches National Park, for example, the completely free-standing Delicate Arch, made from Entrada Sandstone that was first formed around 65 million years ago, stands 65 feet tall and 32 feet wide. Over time, softer rock layers have eroded, leaving behind these harder layers in what looks to be a sculpted masterpiece, so iconic it's featured on Utah's license plates.

It didn't have to be this way. It didn't have to be stunning, elegant, and beautiful. And yet it is.

Nestled into Vermilion Cliffs National Monument is another masterpiece of elements and time. The Wave was formed by wind erosion that has shaped the Navajo Sandstone for the last 190 million years, creating a swirling, vibrant palette of reds, oranges, and pinks.

It didn't have to be this way. It didn't have to be stunning, elegant, and beautiful. And yet it is.

"What in God might appear to us as 'play' is perhaps what He Himself takes most seriously," Thomas Merton writes in *New Seeds of Contemplation*. "At any rate the Lord plays and diverts Himself in the garden of His creation, and if we could let go of our own obsession with what we think is the meaning of it all, we might be able to hear His call and follow Him in His mysterious, cosmic dance. We do not have to go very far to catch echoes of that game, and of that dancing."

I want to follow God into that "mysterious, cosmic dance." On this trip I wanted to be an eyewitness to God's delight, to give my children eyes to see God's whimsy and power and light. I want to be a woman of joy, a woman who treasures these things in her heart, a woman who sighs happily and says "I *love* pine trees!" and laughs along with her teasing children who love her. I want to spend more and more of my time in awe. I want to spend more and more of my time in wonder. I think that's what, perhaps, Thomas Merton was getting at in the meaning of it all—to take God's invitation to enjoy and rejoice in the garden of His creation seriously, to participate as co-choreographers in the celebration of the dance.

But I also need health insurance.

"I know you want to see the road ahead rather than trusting
God. If you continue this way, the road will get longer and
your spiritual progress will slow down. Give yourself as com-
pletely as you can to God. Do so until your final breath, and
He will never desert you."

—François Fénelon, *The Seeking Heart*

Jeremiah and I have a history.

"For I know the plans I have for you," declares the Lord in Jeremiah 29:11, "plans to prosper you and not to harm you, plans to give you hope and a future."

In the infant years of my faith as a college student, discovering this verse and verses like it were simultaneously deeply encouraging and anxiety-producing. As a young person in high school, I had ideas about what I'd like to do as an adult, but when I became a Christian at age eighteen, suddenly a new layer was added to my career pursuits. Now it wasn't just a matter of finding a job I was good at and doing my best at that job. That wasn't enough. I was a follower of Jesus now. What did *God* want me to do?

It seemed like good news to me that *anyone* but especially *God* had a plan for my life. Phew! Thank God someone else is in control of this chaos!

But when was he going to clue me in?! Should I major in this subject, or that subject? Should I teach or should I write or should I try to teach writing? Should I attend this college or transfer to another college? Should I marry this guy, or should I marry some other guy? Should I marry at all? These questions didn't seem to have any clear-cut, God-inspired answers, although I certainly searched and prayed for them. God seemed to be leaving an awful lot up to me.

Then when painful and difficult things began to happen that didn't seem to align with plans that would prosper me, I started to question the truth of Jeremiah 29:11. What was I supposed to do with miscarriages? What was I supposed to do with cancer diagnoses? What was I supposed to do with all of the bad things happening—to me, around me, in the world at large? I wasn't the first to ask such a question, of course. Job, the sad and tortured man in the oldest book in the Bible, wrestled with the question of suffering 3,500 years ago. In all that time, no one has sufficiently found an answer, or at least not one that is especially satisfying when you are smack-dab in the middle of injustice and suffering.

Throughout my twenties, I read Jeremiah 29:11 as a personal promise. But as that personal Plan and Purpose started to erode, I learned that the prophet Jeremiah was speaking to the nation of Israel in that passage. Every "you" was "you plural," not "you singular." We the People. Not Me the Person. God seemed to be concerned with all of humanity's progression toward healing, reconciliation, and peace, not just my particular path, my day-in-and-day-out life choices.

He just wanted me to live, and live abundantly.[11]

That reality released the grip anxiety had on my particular plans and purpose. I didn't need to take Jeremiah's words as a very specific, tactical plan that I may miss or screw up. The plans God has are universe-sized, plans to reconcile all of humanity to God, plans for love and joy and hope and peace and every other good thing. Right?

Even though I thought I abandoned my faith in the God of My Plan and Purpose, try as I might, I haven't been able to stop grasping at whatever signs I can find, trying to prophesy God's particular road map for my life.

Maybe that's okay. Maybe when bad things started to happen, I overcorrected by scoffing at the Hobby Lobby signs proclaiming God's Plan and Purpose, discarding the personal and particular for the universal God. The more I have slowed down and looked for God's hand, the more I have seen God's signature of love written into every living

---

11 John 10:10.

and nonliving thing. God speaks through my gut's tightening in anxiety. God whispers an all-consuming love in the careful balance of the moon's pull on the planet, the tide's ebb and flow, my own cycle of monthly seasons, and our continent's quarterly shifts in weather. Hasn't God seemed to care and provide for me in the "you singular" way while also loving deeply y'all? Hasn't God been in the details as well as the grand plan?

After all, this is what I believe for my children and my husband, too, that God deeply cares about them and wants them to experience that love and constant compassion. I believe that God has a purpose for their lives that is both grand and mundane, ordinary and extraordinary, the natural and supernatural layered together, universal and particular, their deep gladness intersecting with the world's deep need. Maybe there is no one right particular Plan and Purpose, but also, maybe we can take detours, wrong turns, and redirects that lead us away from the better way.

As I talked with Steven back in Boise, the first true doubts about my new job surfaced. Had I made a mistake? Did God *actually* have a plan and a purpose, a particular path he'd paved especially for me? Was this new opportunity an exit ramp off the good and real and true and beautiful plan? Now that I had taken the position and started sharing about my job change, I seemed to be met with a lot of skeptical faces asking a dozen different ways, "Are you sure about this, Sarah?" Was taking this job at Ashland the right choice?

It was too late now. I was starting the Monday after we came home. If I just reduced the workload with all of my clients, I reasoned, I could do this full-time gig and still keep up with the people I'd developed such great relationships with since I left my last job. In the end, I'd probably earn the same or maybe even more than I had been able to make as a freelancer. And we'd have *insurance!* This *seemed* like the direction God had opened for us, to make a way for Brandon to pursue his seminary education and for me to provide for our family. It felt like the right thing to do.

So why wasn't I able to talk about the job without sighing, as if it was already wearing me out just thinking about it? Where was my deep gladness?

"I'll give it three months and see how it's going. It'll be fine," I told Steven. It'll be fine. Just fine. It'll be fine.

> *"Most people don't really know God. They know what they have read, or been told, but it is an intellectual knowledge that lacks true spiritual experience. Most of us grow up being told there is a God, but I'm not sure how much we believe it. We don't act like we believe in God. And those who believe in God have a relationship based on fear rather than love."*
>
> —François Fénelon, *The Seeking Heart*

We did not rise early enough to catch any changing rays of light above Sunrise Point, but let's be honest, I left my disappointment and expectations of keeping to the original Plan back in Indiana. Jesus was smirking at me in front of the Lake Michigan "Coastline Is Closed" sign all the way back on day one. I've tried to learn to belly laugh with him at myself, especially on this trip. *Oh, you silly, adorable daughter*, I imagine him saying. *Come here and give me a smooch.*

Okay, that last bit is definitely something my grandfather used to say to me that I guess now I'm going to attribute to my Laughing Jesus. Grandpa Jesus had the most bristly face!

Maybe that's why so few people can picture God laughing. All kinds of Christian psychologists have noted that our earliest understanding of God is rooted in our relationship with our earthly fathers. But if our earthly fathers were distant, serious, and authoritarian, it could be difficult to imagine a heavenly Father as intimate, compassionate, and joyful, no matter how hard we want him to be that way. I love my dad, and I know that my dad loves me, but there were a lot of years when he seemed far away, busy, and preoccupied making a living. Those years are broken up by moments with him that were so poignant and distinct their memories are now intense, filled with an ache of both love and longing, even still, at age forty.

I didn't try very hard to make my dad laugh as a kid—I was too busy trying to earn his approval instead—but it is one of my favorite sounds, a bursting barrel of joy when it erupts.

"There once was a man with a wooden eye . . ." Dad would begin, a twinkle in his own as he leaned forward toward the campfire.

It is not surprising to me now that our ideas of Father God come from our interactions with our earthly fathers. If you think long enough about how God said he made each of us in his image, then when we look to our fathers (and mothers and sisters and brothers) we ought to see the face of God. It's just that sometimes, the image of God in them is obscured by brokenness, trauma, bitterness, and neglect. The image of God is there, underneath the unhealed wounds. We're all walking around in human jumpsuits, hiding the image of God in our hearts. Most of us don't even know it's there.

I see the image of God in my dad when he is the protector and provider, when he seeks to make a way for his children and grandchildren, when the anxiety and fear are able to melt away for a minute and he can say with tenderness, "I love you, I'm so proud of you." I see it in my mom when she delivers dinner to a friend just because or sends a care package to my kids just because, when she laughs until she cries, and when she shows up with abundant love for people who have been genuinely unlovable in return. I could go on, of course, rattling through each and every person I've ever met, but we don't have enough pages for that.

Sometimes you have to look hard for it, and sometimes it's right in front of you, head tipped back and laughing. Everywhere you look, there's someone wearing the face of God.

Bryce Canyon was another park we took the time to hike when I was a kid. I was the videographer for that part of the trip, and although the footage is shaky and unwatchable, I can picture the trail now through the viewfinder of our camcorder. We were all in summer clothes, dressed for a hot day in Utah's desert landscape in July. My dad wore a T-shirt, blue jeans, and work boots, like he always did. My brothers wedged themselves in hollowed-out caves, tunnels, and tenuous-looking rock formations and asked to have their pictures taken. I narrated the whole time, as if you couldn't see the footage with your own eyes (which you really couldn't because the camera was shaking so badly). "Wow," I said. "Look at those rocks." Wobble wobble wobble. At the end, we hiked up a long zigzag trail of switchbacks out of the canyon. After our hike, we stopped at one more overlook and gazed down upon the amphitheater of tall, thin spires of rock, marveling at the masterpiece before us.

"They're called 'hoodoos,'" I told the kids after we left Pinewoods Resort and parked the truck. We were at the trailhead for the Queen's Garden Trail to the Navajo Loop, starting from Sunrise Point. The world looked handcrafted, perfect to the point of artificiality. The sky was a bright blue with bubbly white cumulus pillows floating in it, straight out of the wallpaper in Andy's room in *Toy Story*, and the hoodoos glowed orange and pink and white against the backdrop of that sky. We looked down on the valley of thousands of rock formations, eerie and mysterious, spiritual spires rising dramatically from the canyon floor. Nowhere else in the world are there so many different types of hoodoos.

When God gave people the ability to name all of creation, I bet he couldn't wait for them to land on these mystical spires. God must have so much fun listening to us come up with new sound combinations to describe and name what he brought into being. I wonder if he has a name for every mineral and creature and person, a name only he knows, but he sits back and delights anyway, listening to us invent new ways to describe what has always been.

"Okay, pals, what name are you going to slap on *these* babies?" Laughing Jesus said. "The Paiute people called them *Angka-ku-wass-a-wits*, or 'red painted faces.' They thought they were ancient people who had been turned to stone for their misdeeds. Who do *you* say they are?"

When Lydia was just learning language, one of her favorite activities was coloring with sidewalk chalk. For years, rather than using "sidewalk chalk," she referred to it as "chidewalking."

"Want to chidewalk?" Yes, I do, always and forever. I'm nominating this term for the next edition of the *Merriam-Webster Dictionary*. If God gets hoodoos, I want chidewalk.

The days of chidewalking are over. Instead, our play takes us onto golf courses and into forests. We laugh at quotes from favorite movies and TV series or our family's shared inside jokes. Brandon and I used to just laugh at the things they said and did, but now, they are old enough to laugh with us, or better yet, at us. Who do they think they are?!

Oh yes, our children. Oh yes, the children of Laughing Jesus.

"Looks like it might rain soon," Brandon said, eyeing the clouds on the canyon horizon.

"It's not going to rain today!" I chirped happily. "And if it does, the weather app says it'll only be two-hundredths of an inch—a light sprinkle! It'll feel refreshing!"

We hiked down into Bryce Canyon, weaving in and out, taking photos through arches and next to lookouts over the vast canyon. A rock like a raised fist protruded from one canyon wall while others stood in rows as if in a large cathedral. Henry carried his walking stick and climbed up into every crevice he could reach. So did Elvis. So did Lydia. Elvis gave me two thumbs up as he walked through a tunnel. I took pictures of trees growing out of rock and flowers growing out of rock and small tufts of grass growing out of rock and thought about resilience and perseverance, beauty and barrenness.

It took a lot of love and suffering to get here. Wrapped inside our marriage there were four miscarriages, NICU visits, chronic illnesses, years of loneliness, shattered trust, career changes, church crises, mental and emotional and spiritual distress, all hard winds that wore away softer rock, eroding us down and shaping us into who we really are.

It didn't have to be this way. It didn't have to be stunning, elegant, and beautiful. And yet it is.

Our three living children walked and talked together in front of Brandon and me, through the sandy paths and pine groves. Near the estimated middle of our hike, we stopped to eat the lunch I packed.

"This is touching all my love languages," I told Brandon, my eyes brimming with tears, as usual, because all I do now is weep at the majesty and miracles happening around me. Listen, cicadas! Tears. Look, a lizard! Tears. My people walking together in front of me on the trail! Tears.

"I still think it's going to rain," Brandon said.

We started the long, sweaty, breathless climb back out of the canyon. I paused for a break and took a photo of more hoodoos on the horizon, in front of a growing patch of dark clouds.

"No," breath, "it isn't," breath, "it's just," breath, "going to," breath, "sprinkle."

I had to stop for a break again, feeling old and lame but trying to remind myself that this was all POTS' fault. Behind us, the sky was that same *Toy Story* blue and white, but to the northwest, it was dark.

"It's probably moving north," I said and refreshed the weather app again. "See? Still two-hundredths of an inch. That's nothing. It's going to miss us."

"See?" Brandon said, pointing to the sky. "I don't need no weather app to tell me if it's going to rain."

It started to drip a little as we made our last turn out of the canyon, up to Sunset Point. We took a few final photos. The drips turned to drops, more frequent, heavier. Brandon began to walk faster. Drops became rain bullets, heavy plunks that stung as they hit our skin. We sprinted the rest of the way to the truck as the sky opened up.

We began the next four hours of our drive to Moab, Utah, with the rain pouring down in staccato beats the wipers couldn't keep up with, like uncontrollable, contagious laughter.

"Guess it isn't going to rain, Mom," the kids mocked from the back seat.

I used to take myself a lot more seriously. Once as a middle school student, I stumbled going up stairs, and a couple of girls behind me laughed. It stung. "Geez!" I said, as if it was their fault I tripped. "*We* didn't do anything!" they replied. I felt sick.

When you take yourself too seriously, there's never an occasion to laugh at yourself. *No heart? No heart?! I'm all heart!* Maybe instead of comparison, arrogance and insecurity are the thieves of joy. They are two sides to the same coin—neither allows us to love ourselves as we are.

If arrogance and insecurity are thieves, the giver of joy is gratitude. When I trust that what God said about me (and everyone else) is true, then I can rest in the reality of being a treasured child of God, knowing that my existence alone is enough; I am loved.

That sure sounds great, but do I really believe it?

> *"Dear Child of God, you are loved with a love that nothing*
> *can shake, a love that loved you long before you were created,*
> *a love that will be there long after everything has disappeared.*
> *You are precious, with a preciousness that is totally quite*
> *immeasurable. And God wants you to be like God. Filled with*
> *life and goodness and laughter—and joy."*

—Archbishop Desmond Tutu, *The Book of Joy*

Utah unfolded its vastness to us around every bend along the four-hour drive from Bryce to Moab. While the boys and I had been used to saying "WOW" every few minutes for almost two weeks, it was all new and overwhelming to Lydia and Brandon. There was so much space, so much endless space, pillars and canyons and open expanses of red, dotted with stout patches of grass, all changing drastically from one moment to the next, with hardly a human in sight besides those few who were driving the highway with us.

"I'm just in awe of God's creation," Lydia reflected from the back seat. The smell of sagebrush seeped into the truck.

Come here and give me a smooch! The delighted Father swings open the door to the playground of the world and says, *I made this for you. Let's go have some fun, shall we?*

To Know and Be Known

Bryce Canyon, July 24, 2022

I can see the tread marks from sneakers
I once wore here. Who wouldn't want to wander
once more through hoodoos, watch their
offspring spring from cliff to tunnel
and inch too close to the edge, an impulse
I wedged in the DNA I gave you? If I fell
it would be into this amphitheater
of wonder where I would spend eter-
nity in wonder at these wonders,
but luckily for me, I stand rapt instead
in the glow of your unfolding. This red
sandstone cathedral is a thread
between what was and is and is yet to be.
The hoodoos promise me the more we
wear away, the clearer we can hear the beat
of what makes us. I want this most of all,
for wind and water to erode you raw,
to know what hides behind your walls.

Chapter 10

GPS to the Presence of God

In order for us to move beyond our utility, we need to stop re-garding as the center of our being what we do to be useful and recognize that who we are in relationship to the center, God, is more important.

—Makoto Fujimura

My itinerary called for another national park on the same day as Bryce. The Plan was to get to Moab about late afternoon, make a quick, two- or three-hour drive through Arches National Park, grab a late dinner, and then go back into the park to catch the sunset through Delicate Arch. I had every intention of seeing that license plate arch in person.

The longer we drove, however, the less enthusiastic the rest of our passengers seemed to be about spending any more time in the truck.

"What do you think?" I asked Brandon. "My itinerary says it takes about two hours or so to drive through the loop."

Brandon made a face. "I don't know."

I chewed on my lip. When would we ever be in Moab again? Maybe never? I sighed.

We drove on in silence, listening to music and taking in the empty scenery. *I bet we could swing through a small bit of the park before dinner, and then after dinner, we could go back. I bet the sunset is amazing over Delicate Arch if you're positioned just right.* I imagined Arches empty except for us, like Yellowstone was as the boys and I delayed leaving that last night, chasing down one more scenic overlook, one more view of the rainbow, one more moment under a changing sunset. Even if we skipped the before-dinner drive, the after-dinner park visit promised to be perfect.

What a memory I had invented; how could we possibly miss it?!

"Why don't we check in at the hotel, check out the pool, and then see how we feel?" I suggested, secretly conspiring to fit in *one more thing.*

"Sounds like a plan!" Brandon said with a laugh.

I know I've already talked about long-COVID and quitting my job so I could recover, but just in case I haven't belabored the point enough yet, I've never been good at resting. You have to understand just how deeply the German Farmer Work Ethic of my father is ingrained in my genetic code. An old neighbor of ours used to cluck his tongue and say, "She's a worker!" as I hauled mulch and pruned shrubs around our front yard, and I grinned with pride.

That's right I am!

Before I was sick, I worked with joyful abandon. I loved my job and my colleagues. I'd stay up late after the kids went to bed working on something *for the fun of it.* Before I was sick, when I wasn't working my paid job, I worked on other projects around the house or on my latest book project. Rest was laziness. When my husband reclined on the couch to watch football on Sundays or closed his eyes for a long afternoon nap on a Saturday, I was annoyed. Why relax when you could collect firewood, plant a garden, go for a hike, plan a party, go out to eat, lead a Bible study, and so on?

And trust me, there was always an "and so on" to tack onto that list.

Rest never came easy to me because rest was not a virtue I was taught. I was taught to work hard. I counted my life as valuable by what I was contributing, by what I had worked for and earned. I was a human doing, not a human being.

After my POTS diagnosis, it took a forty-five-day-long migraine to make me resign from my job. Maybe I could have taken a leave of absence to recover, but I didn't know if I would ever recover. Quitting my job was one of the hardest things I have ever done. I wasn't leaving for something else or leaving a place I couldn't tolerate; I left because I couldn't do the work anymore, and that was humiliating. I left because I needed rest.

I needed rest physically so my brain and body could heal, that much I knew. I needed to be able to sleep whenever I felt fatigued, or else the fatigue would spiral into a headache and brain fog and exhaustion, triggering all of the symptoms I was trying so hard to alleviate. COVID gave me a chronic illness that I know how to manage now, because I took the time to focus on recovery. I can, for the most part, predict how my body will respond on any given day based on what I did the night before. It wasn't *really* a surprise that I had a POTS attack in Yellowstone; I could have read all of the signs ahead of time and known it was coming. Without all of that time and space to rest, my body would not have been able to keep going at the pace my regular life required of it.

But there was more to my recovery than I knew. In the wake of my resignation, God completely reframed my existence. I used to think I had to earn my place, and if I hadn't earned my place, I had no right to rest. No longer was I Super Sarah, Director of Content Marketing, Unicorn of the Office, Marvel of the Production Wing. Now I was just Sarah. Just Sarah, who wrote articles from time to time. Just Sarah, who needed to nap every day. Just Sarah, with no titles besides "Brandon's wife" and "Lydia/Elvis/Henry's mom." I was just me, with nothing to point to and say, this is why I'm worth your time. This is why I can take a vacation, or read a book, or watch a movie. This is how I've *earned* my life.

In hindsight, God had a lot of work to do. A pretty gargantuan task, really. I wish that it hadn't taken a life-altering disease for me to understand and accept the gift of rest, otherwise known as Sabbath.

The only way I could learn about rest was through my chronic illness. Franciscan friar Richard Rohr has said that love and suffering are the universal paths God offers to all people to change and reach them— these are the true primary spiritual teachers. During this season, suffering led the lecture in my life.

I didn't anticipate how much spiritual healing God would orchestrate in that time of rest. It was as if he set this message on repeat: *You do not need to prove yourself to me. Rest. You are loved and valued just because* you are. *So rest. You were created by God, in the image of God, called one of God's children, one of God's own, just because. So rest. It is a gift to just exist. So rest.*

I am not a human doing; I am a human being.

Rest is one of the very first mandates God gives to humanity. He modeled it for us in the narrative of creation by resting on the seventh day.[12] It is so important that God made it one of the Ten Commandments, "but the seventh day is a sabbath to the Lord your God. On it you shall not do any work, neither you, nor your son or daughter, nor your male or female servant, nor your animals, nor any foreigner residing in your towns. For in six days the Lord made the heavens and the earth, the sea, and all that is in them, but he rested on the seventh day. Therefore the Lord blessed the Sabbath day and made it holy."[13]

The Old Testament extended Sabbath rest to the natural world as well.[14] Once every seven years, the earth needed to rest from production, to regenerate soil, to sigh and be enriched. Every seventh Sabbath year cycle, or every fiftieth year, was supposed to be a jubilee, when everything was set free and everything equalized, including land rights.

"The land must not be sold permanently, because the land is mine and you reside in my land as foreigners and strangers," God said.

---

12 Genesis 2:2.
13 Exodus 20:10–11.
14 Leviticus 25:3–5.

"Throughout the land that you hold as a possession, you must provide for the redemption of the land."[15]

In our buzzing, busy, driven society, God's old-school Sabbath rule seems antiquated and unproductive. But when you live a Sabbath-defined life, you allow yourself, your neighbors, your family, and all of creation to dwell for a day or time in the kingdom of the Living God, just as they are, just because they exist.

No demands are put on performance during the Sabbath, only rest, only nourishing the spirit. Sabbath is restoration.

In his book *Sabbath as Resistance: Saying No to the Culture of Now*, theologian Walter Brueggeman wrote, "Sabbath is the celebration of life beyond and outside productivity." On this side of suffering, with all the tools I need to manage my illness, it is far easier for me to say no to the demands that insist I need to produce more instead of just producing enough. It is far easier now for me to say yes to rest, to time richly spent in relationship, in the outdoors, in prayer, or asleep with my dogs on the couch at three in the afternoon. But it's also still easy to give in to the temptation of the old ways, to return to the hamster wheel of performance and productivity.

When I was first recovering, I had no choice except to rest or risk being depleted down to nothing; now, I have to choose.

Our culture tends to view rest as a luxury. Like me, most of us think we need to earn a break. But Sabbath rest isn't nice to take when you have the time; it's a *benevolent commandment*, good and necessary for a flourishing world, like the rest of the commandments. It's a generous gift to intentionally stop what you are doing and enter with joy into God's presence.

But what does it mean to be in God's presence? Were we in God's presence in the Temple of Sinawava in Zion? What about in the Boise conference center? Which mountain do I have to climb, which cavern

---

15 Leviticus 25:23–24.

do I need to spelunk, which ocean do I need to cross to find the presence of God?

None of them. And all of them.

It isn't like God is hiding. We just don't always have eyes to see or the time it takes to find him. It's like we've closed our eyes to count to ten in a game of eternal hide-and-seek and given up before we got to two. That took too long. Guess I'm never going to find you, O omnipresent Lord of the universe.

In the little and profound book *The Practice of the Presence of God*, Brother Lawrence told his friend, "All we have to do is to recognize God as being intimately present within us." Weirdly referring to himself as someone else in an act of humility, Brother Lawrence continued, "He said his prayers consisted totally and simply of God's presence. His soul was resting in God, having lost its awareness of everything but love of him. When he wasn't in prayer, he felt practically the same way. Remaining near to God, he praised and blessed him with all his strength. Because of this, his life was full of continual joy."

God is always present—if you're looking for him, you can't miss him. He's like the signs promoting Wall Drug throughout South Dakota and surrounding states: they're everywhere. If you're driving fast enough, though, the signs flash by in an instant, and before you know it, you've missed it. And him.

That's why I think God gave us the Sabbath. This commandment of old is even confirmed by trusty ol' science. Rest is baked into our circadian rhythms. Research shows that people who take a planned day of rest each week experience less stress, have better heart health, sleep better, recover faster physically, and actually live longer.

But Sabbath isn't just about physical health. It's about finding your soul restored. "The Sabbath is the presence of God in the world, open to the soul of man," Jewish theologian Abraham Joshua Heschel said in his book *The Sabbath: Its Meaning for Modern Man*. This planned stoppage resets our systems and makes space for us to see the holy in the everyday. When we push against demands to *produce produce produce*, we open up space for more moments in time to experience God. The soul at rest in God is a soul that knows its worth, its foundation, its value. In the restful care of God, the urge to please, to produce, and to perform subsides, eclipsed by the bone-deep peace of knowing who you are, even as you are known.

The rest we gain through one day of Sabbath permeates our moments throughout the week, "like a palace in time with a kingdom for all," Heschel wrote. "It is not a date but an atmosphere."

Now *that's* a satisfying reason to Sabbath.

Heschel also said, "God is not in things of space, but in moments of time," which I for sure starred and underlined. But that doesn't mean I always agree with him.

"You know, this has been a great trip," Brandon said as we drove along the red rock cliffs toward Moab, "but it isn't exactly vacation."

"What do you mean?" I said, immediately offended.

"No, it's great! But it isn't restful. There's a big difference between sightseeing and sitting on a beach somewhere. I think next year, we need to just sit on a beach."

The peanut gallery in the back seat chirped their agreement.

"Yes! The beach! I would *love* to be sitting on the beach right now, for *hours*, just soaking up the sun and listening to the waves," Lydia said.

"And riding the waves," Henry piled on.

"And playing video games inside," Elvis might as well have said, while wearing his headphones and playing video games inside the moving vehicle.

"But this is great, too!" Lydia said.

We drove on quietly for a few minutes, visions of the beach floating in our minds.

"There isn't that much time left with these three, and there's still so much in the world for us to see," I told Brandon once the kids all had their earbuds back in, all the while feeling that same longing for hot sand and cool tidewater pulsing through the pads of my feet.

I wanted to take our family to Sequoia National Park and the Grand Canyon. Elvis wanted to see Vegas and Memphis. Henry had always wished he could have gone to Acadia with Lydia and my mom and me. He also wanted to go back to Kentucky, to the Natural Bridge State Resort Park and our cabin in the woods with the firepit, frozen pizza dinner, and ice cream dessert we ate in the hot tub. And those were just the places we'd already seen; what about all of the places that were yet to be visited—Montana and San Francisco, Oregon and Louisiana, Texas and Hawaii and Alaska? What about the places beyond our borders? I have been to six out of 195 countries. My kids have been to one, this one. There were so many places yet to see.

We had been to the beach again and again, and yes, I *loved* the beach. But time was running out to get to all of the spaces together where I knew the wonders of God were hiding. In two years, Lydia would graduate. In four, so would Elvis. In seven, so would Henry. And then they would be gone. We would be out of time.

There wasn't enough time for a restful beach vacation. There was still too much to do.

I'm not the only one who experienced the revelation of the gift of rest in the wake of the pandemic. So did the planet.

The documentary *The Year Earth Changed* showcased the dramatic and surprising transformation our planet's ecosystem experienced while its dominant species' activity came to a sudden halt in 2020. Within days, cities in the United States experienced the best air quality they'd had in forty years. Hidden for decades by smog in India, after just twelve days, the Himalayas were visible from two hundred kilometers away. Six months after the start of the pandemic lockdown, the Ganges River saw an 80 percent increase in its oxygen levels. Because of COVID, the year 2020 was a mandatory, nonnegotiable jubilee year. Counting backward, the last jubilee year before that would have been 1970, which marked the beginning of the first

Earth Day and the start of the Clean Air Act, leading to decades of policy reform and environmental action.

The pandemic showed us just how much of a role we play in providing redemption for the land, and how even small accommodations can make a big difference.[16] The Scriptures provide us an ancient road map that aligns with modern conservationist practices to cast a vision for a future hope and a restored planet that can sustain flourishing life for hundreds of years to come.

Maybe there could be time to see everything after all.

We continued our drive, rolling along 70 East to 191 South, the miles ticking closer and closer to the entrance to Arches National Park.

In the before-times, I would've forced the issue. I would've looked over at Brandon with big doe eyes and a grin and convinced him of just *one more stop*, and he would've rolled his eyes and gone along with my Plan because he loves me and knows I just can't help myself.

Instead, I took a deep breath and told my restless self, *just stop*.

We passed the entrance to Arches and kept driving.

When mapping out the trip and booking places to stay, I had told myself that everything we saved on the Roughin' It part of our road trip would be spent splurging this last leg, so after hemming and hawing for a couple of days, I finally pressed the checkout button on the Marriott's Element Moab website. *Ka-ching!* The credit card company employees paused their envelope-stuffing campaigns a moment to celebrate one more customer spending more than they should. Woo-hoo, here comes another heaping pile of interest, plenty to pay our Christmas bonuses!

To be fair to me, Moab is not cheap. There aren't exactly rustic options available anyway, and besides, the boys and I *ate peanut butter and jelly sandwiches for days* and *slept in a tent* (one night) to make this happen! We *deserved* the Marriott.

---

16 Leviticus 25:23–24.

"Wow, this place is awesome!" the kids chirped, hauling their dusty bags from the back of the packed truck and tromping into the hotel. "Can we swim?"

The Marriott had a beautiful pool, floating lounge chairs, a hot tub, and elegant canopies with beds inside them. With Arches somewhere in the back of my mind, we changed into swimsuits and made our way down to sit poolside under a late afternoon sky streaked with the occasional wisp of cloud, surrounded by red rocks.

"This," Brandon said, sitting down next to me on a lounge chair, "now *this* is a vacation."

The two of us savored the first few minutes we'd had alone together, watching the kids splash and laugh and roughhouse as only teenagers caught between adulthood and childhood can do. While the kids swam, we talked through the coming changes ahead of us back home. Brandon had doubts about whether he should quit his job. I had doubts about whether I should have taken my new job.

"You absolutely should quit," I told Brandon. "That's the whole reason I took this job."

"I know," he said. "I'm just having a moment."

"Well, stop it," I said with a smile. I told him about my conversation with Steven at the conference and the uncomfortable feeling I had that taking this job might have been a mistake.

"I don't know, maybe God opened this door for you to give me permission to leave my job," he said. "I wouldn't have done it without this safety net, you know."

"Maybe," I said with a sigh. "I'll give it at least three months."

"Yeah, you can always quit."

"Yeah, I guess," I said, *but then I'd be Just Sarah again.* It was time to change the subject. "You know, we could take a drive through Arches at sunset. I bet it'd be beautiful."

Brandon groaned. "I think we all need some time out of the car. We're going to be driving for a long time again tomorrow."

In my mind, I imagined the Delicate Arch and the wonderland of arches on the other side of the park's entrance. For some reason, I pictured it like one of those Christmas light displays you drive through in slow motion, *oohing* and *ahhing* around every turn. There was a Vegas flashing neon sign with a giant arrow that said Arches, pointing toward the magnificent and popular and yet entirely deserted Delicate Arch, waiting just for me. If I just conjured a little more energy, made a little more time, pushed a little farther . . . we could make it happen.

To my left, the kids dove under and surfaced, laughing and splashing, shaking their wet heads and spraying water everywhere.

"You're probably right," I conceded.

One night during our out west trip when I was a kid, we stayed at a hotel with a beautiful pool overlooking Lake Powell. My mom must have splurged on it; it felt luxurious and majestic. The sunset was magnificent. It was one of the highlights of our trip.

Not Lake Powell. The hotel pool. Come on, what kid doesn't love a hotel pool?!

But in the not-so-distant future, I'll ask the kids about the most memorable part of our Wells Out West trip. Was it Bryce? Was it Zion? What about Yellowstone—the views, the bison, the Grand Prismatic Spring?

Inevitably, one of them will say the hotel in Moab.

Why?! Are you saying we could have found a sweet hotel pool in Ohio and had just as much of a memorable experience?

Maybe. Maybe, because our best memories aren't wrapped up in what the humans are doing, but who the humans are being. Yes, the rock formations were amazing. Yes, I want to go and see and do even more, more and more, far into the future. But if our circumstances changed and we could no longer make travel a priority in our family, what binds us is hopefully far more substantive than our shared scrapbook of photographs. Maybe what we remember is the rest, the timbre of our shared laughter, the ease of being exactly ourselves together in this abundant world.

After a mediocre Mexican dinner in Moab and browsing some gift shops, we drove back to the hotel and walked through the parking lot, soaked in another picturesque sunset over red-faced rock walls. The clouds across the sky were silver and gray against a navy blue backdrop, a sky to rival the ceiling of the Sistine Chapel. It was a sky that promised a long night of rest instead of stargazing.

"No clear sky of stars tonight," I told Brandon as I snapped a few photos of the otherworldly sunset. *This is it for opportunities to see the world beyond our world,* I thought to myself.

And it is well. The following night, we planned to stay with friends in Denver. Then, we'd head to St. Louis, and from there, home.

For now, a good night's rest.

On the Train Down Pikes Peak, God Answers the Prayer to See More Wildlife

Pikes Peak, Colorado

No, I don't
ask the moose
to perform
in the lake
as it drinks
or the elk
to appear
on demand
for one more
train filled with
bipedal
images
of Me. Quit
holding your
smartphone up
to capture
a snapshot.
You have no
lens to see.
Mother Moss
warms boulders,
the black-eyed
Susans wink
among the
wild grasses,
conifers
hum needles
together,
"Shh, listen,"

the aspen
grove whispers
through its one
root system,
my inchworm
crawls above
a billion
microor-
ganisms
who sing a
perfect song
of humus
in this dark
night. Don't ask
me one more
time. I have
already
given more
than you can
ever name.

Chapter II

Country Roads Take Me Home

*I'm thanking you, God, from a full heart, I'm writing the book
on your wonders. I'm whistling, laughing, and jumping for joy;
I'm singing your song, High God.*

—Psalm 9:1–2 MSG

The kids didn't know it, but we had a four o'clock ticket for the Broadmoor Manitou and Pikes Peak Cog Railway to ride to the summit of Pikes Peak, which meant we had to say goodbye to Moab by eight a.m. that morning. The drive from Utah to Colorado just kept getting more awe-inspiring with every mile as the red canyon ridges shifted to high mountains coated in evergreens.

Lydia, Elvis, and Henry each put on their headphones and settled in with their various devices, glancing occasionally out the window and muttering, "Wow" in response to whatever we yelled at them to look at from the front seat. It's time to be wonder-struck, children! Meanwhile Brandon and I resumed what has been one of my favorite things about marriage—riding together to some far-off destination, singing along to the radio.

I remember being a child in the back seat on road trips with my parents. Even though we were all in the same car, it was as if a separate world existed in the front row from what was happening in the back. In

171

the back seat, we watched *Toy Story* and *The Muppet Christmas Carol* and recorded episodes of *Looney Tunes* on the portable TV/VCR. I kept a running tally of the state license plates we passed as my dad's lead foot propelled us down the interstate. I made my brothers play the alphabet game, hunting for words on billboard signs that began with X for miles and miles. "Just find *any* X!" my mom would finally call out. As luck would have it, we'd pass the E**x**it for Beckle**y** Travel Pla**z**a and then the game would end. I was dimly aware that my parents still existed there in the front seat, talking quietly, or not talking at all, always with some country music station playing Garth Brooks, George Strait, Reba McEntire, or Shania Twain, perhaps switching over for a time to Tom Petty or Buck Owens cassette tapes.

I've been riding in the front seat with my husband now for twenty years, exactly half my life, having met him the summer I turned twenty. We are the ones talking quietly underneath the melody of singer-songwriters. We are the ones who choose the artists and navigate through the stations.

As we flipped through SiriusXM Radio channels along the route across Colorado, "I'm Like a Bird" by Nelly Furtado came on. Brandon tried to keep scanning, but I made him go back. He rolled his eyes but obliged. I began to sing along, staring out the window at the sharp-edged cliffs so high I couldn't see their tops.

Brandon didn't know the girl who needed that song in Australia in 2001. I had sung the chorus at the top of my lungs, feeling every note in my gut. We sped along the highway with the windows down, riding on the wrong side of the road in my American mind. Eric, my boyfriend at the time, was in the driver's seat as we drove the Great Ocean Road in search of the Twelve Apostles, the rock formations that line the coast of southern Australia 170 miles west of Melbourne. Wind whipped my hair across my face as I marveled at the changing shades of gold and orange on the rocks.

Everywhere I looked on that trip I saw signs: the Southern Cross in the night sky, Twelve Apostles calling to me in the fading light, a woman speaking words of comfort over me in her foreign tongue, all colliding with the haunting feeling I probably ought not be with Eric. I blamed God.

I was in love. For so long I had wanted to be loved.

Nelly and I sang loudly, meaningfully, prophetically. I knew in my heart I'd fly away one day, away from that guy. But right then I still felt like my soul, my *home*, was there, with Eric.

That girl was the skeletal formation of the young woman Brandon met at church a year later, a woman tired of allowing herself to be defined by the men she was with and eager to stand in her own identity.

When Brandon and I met, the ghosts from both our former relationships followed us in many forms but mostly chose to haunt our CD stacks. I refused to listen to any more Jimmy Buffett. I avoided "3AM" by Matchbox Twenty and bit my lip a little whenever I heard George Strait sing "Run" or Tim McGraw belt out "Take Me Away from Here." Just one line of one verse would draw me back into the dusty cab of Eric's truck, onto his boat, into his bed. I would close my eyes and try to blink away the memory, angry he'd seared himself so fully into my skin. Brandon had his own set of off-limits songs, including Dave Matthews Band's entire catalog. We never questioned each other about what happened to cause whole genres of music to be relegated to shoeboxes crammed into closets. We just knew.

Nelly Furtado finished her final cycle through the chorus and Brandon gladly changed the station, turning to his modern-day hero, James McMurtry. In a flash I slid back into the front seat of our Ford F-150, Eric replaced by my husband, singing along with McMurtry about losing his glasses and how we can't make it here anymore. As James McMurtry ended his lament about the Middle East war, Brandon turned to the Dave Matthews Band channel, then over to Margaritaville. It may have taken twenty years, but we can do it now.

"I never realized until the last few years just how spiritual Dave Matthews's music is," I said.

I've thought many different ways about those past relationships since Brandon and I met, emotions washing together and collecting in a tide pool of embarrassment and longing, regret and anger, grief and relief. But I have been with my husband now for longer than I have not.

George and Tim and Dave and Jimmy and everything their songs represented for us didn't wreck us. They formed us for each other.

Nothing was wasted.

Somewhere between Moab and Manitou Springs we landed on the familiar Kenny Chesney song "Come Over."

"Baby climbing walls," Brandon muttered, and we laughed at the shared memory of our children, much younger then, hearing the song. They thought the idea of a baby climbing walls was hilarious.

That's what *they* remembered, but *I* remembered playing *Welcome to the Fishbowl* on repeat with them in the back seat when I drove from Ashland to Mansfield or Ashland to Auburn or Ashland to Akron, always without Brandon. "Come Over" was the first song on the album. It was year nine-going-on-ten of our marriage when *Welcome to the Fishbowl* was released. Lydia was six, Elvis was five, Henry was one, Brandon was at the peak of traveling with ESPN, I had a troubling relationship with a colleague, and I didn't know what I was doing with any of them. There were so many songs on that album that filled me with longing and loneliness, and I would ache and weep as I drove home from the bookstore, from my grandma's house, from the farm, missing my husband.

"Baby climbing walls," Elvis chuckled from his car seat. Lydia giggled with him.

I still just wanted to be loved. Why was that so hard?

Welcome to the Fishbowl marked the end of an era. Soon after that, CDs gave way to MP3s, and then the Cloud came with its shared music and subscription services and playlists. Before you could access any music anywhere in the world at any time of day, I uploaded dozens of CDs we owned, including the double live James Taylor album and John Hiatt's greatest hits. To combat the loneliness, remind myself that I loved my husband, and ready myself for his return, I started a "Night Music" playlist I packed with songs from our early days and other new favorites. Eric Church's "Like a Wrecking Ball" followed "Feels Like

Rain" by John Hiatt, and I closed my eyes, waiting for the garage door to open so I could greet my husband, hungry.

During that season, concerts reconnected us to our pre-children selves. They helped us to remember who we were together and why we loved each other in the first place, so we booked as many shows as we could, taking off to see the artists who had taken residence in our playlists since the beginning of our relationship.

I never imagined that my life would be so defined by music, even though so many of my favorite childhood memories involved aunts and grandparents playing instruments. They played the piano and the guitar, the mandolin and the accordion, and they sang with the most beautiful variation of voices and harmonies. Brandon didn't play any instruments when we met, and I played only the clarinet, which isn't exactly the first instrument you think of when you say, "Hey, let's sit around and have someone play some music!" Despite our lack of musical talent, music mattered to Brandon and me, and that was enough.

Then one Christmas I bought him an amp and a twelve-string guitar. It was at the beginning of some brittle years in our marriage. I was giddy with excitement to give him those gifts. *This* would be the gift to top all gifts. Lydia knew what was coming and helped me drag the boxes from the back of the tree. She was just as giddy as me.

"This one first, and then that one," I directed, wanting him to open the guitar first.

Wearing pajama pants, a sweatshirt, and a skullcap and sitting in a garage sale chair, Brandon slowly opened up the guitar.

"Wow," he said. "This is unexpected."

I can't be sure, but I think that's when our life together began its slow turning, as John Hiatt calls it. We were still in the midst of a loving and yet static-filled storm, with more dark clouds coming on the horizon, but most nights, Brandon practiced. Brandon practiced all afternoon with our friend Tim while our kids ran around the yard together. I came home from work to "Harvest Moon" harmonies and the two of them learning the chords for "The Circle Game." He wrote the first few verses and chords to a song called "American Honey" and gave them to me for our tenth anniversary.

Brandon practiced in his grandmother's living room after we moved away from Ashland into the wilderness season. He sang and strummed in Grandma's rose pink chairs, gazing out the front window beside the fireplace, wondering what would happen when he quit traveling with ESPN. He jammed with a friend in our basement, tracked down open mics, and found live karaoke nights while I commuted between Cleveland and then Ashland for work and wrote some books, wondering what would happen next.

After Brandon quit ESPN, while my mom was in the early stages of cancer treatments and our children were still under the age of ten, there was the long stretch of time when I questioned if all this work was worth it. We had weathered a lot together, but was a shared history and a regular rotation of concerts enough to keep us together? I added "These Days" by Jackson Browne to my Night Music playlist, then "Colder Weather" by Zac Brown Band, then "I Hold On" by Dierks Bentley. Maybe we were just two different people, too different to justify spending the rest of our lives together. Wouldn't it be easier to just put up a wall between us instead of trying to understand each other better again?

There was no guarantee that things weren't going to fall apart at any moment, but I had to trust that they might just hold. I hoped they would. Sometimes all you can do is hang on to the substance of things hoped for. "I. Hold. On," I crooned with Dierks Bentley, staring at Brandon, holding my hands in fists against my chest, mockingly and with deepest sincerity. We held on, walking Izzy and our marriage through the wilderness season.

When we moved back to Ashland, he transformed our new basement into a music studio, installing sound panels in the drop ceiling and inviting friends to play every Sunday evening while I read or wrote above, feeling the thrum of the bass and the drums vibrate through the floor. "We're Alright Now" by John Hiatt got added to Night Music, alongside Chris Stapleton's "More of You." The guys became a band and the band booked gigs and our lives took on a new kind of rhythm: no more weekend work trips, only Friday and Saturday night gigs.

And when the world shut down, we hammered out the words and chords to songs that didn't exist before, the two of us making music and lyrics, like that Hugh Grant and Drew Barrymore movie, and it was as intimate as the work it took to create our three children. Because of the strange ways COVID had affected our family while the rest of our community thought it was all hype, the pandemic felt like the two of us alone against the world, taking risks and standing up and speaking out, practicing integrity in ways that hadn't been required of us previously. Isolation, both physical and philosophical, bonded us even closer. I added Eric Church's "Hell of a View" to the Night Music playlist. We're not for everybody, either.

"What if you try . . ." I'd say, suggesting a different turn of phrase while sautéing onions, and he'd adjust the rhyme, strum the rhythm, sing the line. Original music that we wrote together flowed between us, filling me with desire and delight.

Years earlier I attended a poetry conference in West Chester, Pennsylvania. One of the nights someone hosted an after-party. An older woman poet was asked to sing—just sing, anything, right there in the front foyer—and she *did*, she just lifted her arms and started belting out a song. I stood against the wall and couldn't believe that people could be that sure of themselves. I was in my mid-twenties with a couple babies at home. A lot of life was about to happen to me.

Now, Brandon and his band are a regular act on the outdoor patio of a local bar. He sings some covers and a few of our originals, including "Long Winter," a pandemic love song and the first one we wrote together. By now, it's routine, the way he stands up there, the way he plays, the way he sings. His presence is magnetic. We make eye contact as he sings a line that we've laughed about sitting around our kitchen island and I can't stop smiling. *It is just you and me, me and you, husband.*

These years since he opened up that guitar have pulled back some protective layer that had been over my husband since before we ever met, revealing more of the man I married to me. Twenty years in, and there's still more I'm getting to know, more ways he is changing, more ways he is being shaped and formed, and I get to be in the front seat. Of course, he isn't the only one being shaped and formed. Maybe he feels the same way I do. Maybe he steals a glimpse of me reclining on the couch with the dogs and a book and can't help but think, *God, I'm so grateful.* I mean, look at me in these flannel pajamas, greasy hair, knit socks, and Tree Hugger hat. Who wouldn't be grateful?

I know it may not always be this way. It was not this way when I lamented to a girlfriend that I didn't think we'd make it, when I day-dreamed about apartments on the east side of Cleveland. In a few years, all of our children will be adults, and where will we be then? This season is one of relative peace and ease after a long stretch of gains, but we can see the shadows of the approaching season of loss on the horizon—losing aunts, losing uncles, the ruthless promise of losing parents, losing health, losing friends, losing more loved ones. What will that season look like? How will we be changed and shaped? When and who will need us? How suddenly or slowly will that happen?

These questions used to be so much more pressing when my mom's cancer was a looming shadow of mortality instead of the miraculous cure we are able to mostly abide in, save for the weeks leading up to six-month follow-up scans. We've been able to push those fears and questions to the gravelly shoulder of the road most hours of the day, but they're still there, unhelpful.

There is only one way to push back the fears about the next years of our lives. I must hold it all loosely, open, in the palms of my hands, and have faith. All I know for sure is that because we held on to a little evidence of things unseen, so far, we've gotten to witness our collective becoming. Others have not been so lucky. I simply do not know what or when or how it will all go, but I trust that it will all be held. It will all be brought together, restored, unified, and rejoiced over. It is already held. These are the best years, these and those and the next and the ones that come after it.

Brandon flipped the station to one with The Rolling Stones singing "Beast of Burden." It was the song we had picked for the garter removal tradition at our wedding. There he is, doing his best Mick

Jagger impression, puckering his lips, strutting and singing, and there I am, blushing and grinning at my new husband as he slips his hands up my dress and modestly removes the white lace. And there we were on the highway, visiting these different versions of ourselves as we trekked across the country, introducing our new selves to our old selves again. Brandon puckers up all over, one hand on the wheel and the other on his hip.

Brandon's quite good at Mick Jagger, but I like it best when he sings *our* songs, with *his* voice. There's only one voice like it.

I guess you never really know what to expect when you marry a person. That's part of the adventure. But I really didn't expect marriage to free us up so much, to simultaneously anchor us and release us to soar. When you have a person who gives you permission to be your real self, what can stand in your way? Nothing.

We arrived at Pikes Peak with a wedge of time to park and climb to the train's boarding platform.

"I don't think it's going to rain," the kids said to me as it started to rain.

The train climbed up the mountain as far as the fog and rain would allow before slowly going back down. Driving across the country had been eye-opening, but this crawl through the wilderness was a whole other experience. I often forget that there are more mountains beyond the mountains that border the road we're driving. This stretch of mountains just wraps itself around the highway like the blurred edge of a map, with nothing more to offer on the other side. Instead, of course, there's more, far more than we can even fathom.

Afterward we stayed in Denver with Chris and Tiffany. I met Chris the same week I met Brandon, going to lunch with the two of them after church. A couple of weeks after we met, Chris started dating Tiffany. We all got married within a month of each other.

As we drove toward Estes Park the next day, Chris told our kids the story of how he wasn't going to leave the church parking lot until their dad chased me down and asked me out to lunch. The two of them reminisced, telling and retelling the stories that made us, our children interjecting questions as we rode along. The kids call it "Dad Lore." I call it "BS," before Sarah.

I used to babysit their son in the afternoons after school. That same son is in the Air Force now. Chris and Tiffany are a couple of steps ahead of us in life, empty nesting with home renovation projects and trips to The Villages in Florida. We're just beginning to imagine what that future will be like. I spent the first few years of our marriage desperate to fill it with children, and then they were there, filling it. Soon they won't be the main focal point of our relationship. As we turn toward the next years, what will sustain us? Probably walking. Maybe traveling. Definitely friendships. Most likely music.

I wondered these things as we listened to Chris and Tiffany talk about their plans for retirement. "You guys should put a deposit on one of the places in The Villages," they pitched to us. "It's crazy. Golf carts everywhere. Live music every night."

When they knew us best, they knew different versions of us, and us of them. They were best acquainted with the George Strait and Chris LeDoux couple, the country line dancing and cowboy boot-wearing couple. Are we those people still, at all? When we walk the dogs, when we sip our coffee, when we write our songs, when we watch our shows, we ask each other if we've read the latest newsletter from Richard Rohr. We quote Arthur Brooks and Julian of Norwich to each other. We ask Alexa to play more Paul Simon and James McMurtry. In response to political strife, we don't play "Beer for My Horses" by Toby Keith and Willie Nelson; instead, we offer our children "I Am a Patriot" by Jackson Browne.

And yet, somewhere inside us is the couple who line danced to George Strait on our second date.

The Plan had been to hike, a lot, in Rocky Mountain National Park, but Chris was our tour guide, and there was so much he wanted us to see—ways and places we wouldn't have known to go. We left it up to him to set the course for our time together and didn't once regret it.

Chris drove us into Estes Park and up into the mountains, guiding and narrating while we hung our heads out the window and gawked at another massive natural masterpiece. We climbed over a rockfall from the '80s or '90s that created a new landscape. We saw a moose bathing in a lake and a bighorn sheep creeping along the valley nearby. We drove through groves of aspen, all clones of each other and interconnected through a shared root system. We drove through evergreen patches that had been eaten by pine beetles, leaving behind the spruce they don't seem to like as much. We drove past acres and acres of wildflowers in bloom for their short season on the tundra before the snow covered them again. We drove by elk grazing and lazing about on steep hillsides.

We drove up and up, until we reached Alpine Visitor Center, 11,796 feet above sea level at Fall River Pass, one mile west of the highest point on Trail Ridge Road. Trail Ridge Road is the highest paved continuous road in the United States. As we drove, Chris tried to find the state flower, columbine, among all of the buttercup and bluebell, St. John's wort and clover, aster and phlox. Eventually we spied some. We worked our way back below the tree line, where the habitat is still harsh, where trees only grow branches on one side of their trunk because of the wind. Even on the tundra, life is adapting.

We exited the park and returned to Estes Park to shop and eat ice cream before we drove away again to our friends' home. On the ride back, the kids were elsewhere, watching reels and chasing bosses and high scores in whatever virtual world they navigated. Brandon and Chris were singing "Big Balls in Cowtown" covered by Waylon Jennings and "Copenhagen" by Chris LeDoux, lost in the front seat to their former selves.

For a moment, I was riding in the back seat of a car in New Zealand, Eric and his best friend in the front. For a moment, I was rolling my eyes and watching my future husband stack beer bottles at the Boot Scoot'n Saloon. For a moment, I was angry he had been out drinking and singing karaoke the night before we moved into our new home in Ashland. For a moment, I was under the cover of shyness, watching other people belt out a song and be their full selves. For a moment, I was alone, singular in this world in which no one can really know the real you, never really know all of the facets that make you, the shadows that threaten you, the lies you listen to, the worries that eat you.

Will it always be this way, I wondered, swinging between different versions of me, distinct and yet tethered to this man, this family, this world.

Somewhere in the night, a voice said, *No*.

The next morning we packed our things into the truck and started the long, flat drive across Kansas toward Ashland. I settled back into the easy familiarity of our family. I love other people, but I also love it when it's just us.

The mountains began to shrink in the rearview mirror. After so many days of new ridges and canyons around every turn, the skyline was only interrupted by telephone wires and wind turbines. The only buildings tall enough to scrape the sky were grain elevators and water towers.

The Plan was to eat dinner and sleep in Kansas City and then head to St. Louis in the morning. Friends back home had insisted that we go to the City Museum.

"It's hard to describe," they had said. "You have to see it to believe it."

As we approached Kansas City late in the afternoon, Brandon said, "Why don't you try to find a place with live music and good BBQ for dinner?"

I opened Google Maps. "Here's a place," I said. "BB's Lawnside Blues and BBQ. There's a band playing there tonight!"

"How far off the highway is it?" he asked, never one to take too long of a detour.

"Just a couple of minutes," I replied.

"Let's do it," Brandon said.

"BBQ and live music tonight, kids!" I said with delight.

During my childhood out west trip, Mom and Dad were determined to stop at Buck Owens' Crystal Palace in Bakersfield, California. My aunt June had made my dad a double cassette dub of Buck Owens that played on repeat throughout my teens. Buck Owens meant something to him. We arrived at the Crystal Palace when nothing much was really happening. Buck Owens' was out somewhere on tour, I suppose. We walked around and looked at the walls full of photos, and then left, heading back into the desert. Years later my dad would call me late in the night eastern time and leave a long and incoherent voicemail from a buzzing Crystal Palace.

"Sare, we're at Buck Owens' Crystal Palace, and this girl is singing," he said. "Listen."

I tried to listen, over and over, begging the muffled audio to clear out so that I could hear what he was trying to tell me.

I couldn't hear it then. But I know, now.

We rolled into BB's Lawnside Blues and BBQ and grabbed red vinyl chairs along the rows of tables covered in red and white checkered tablecloths. From the ceiling hung flying pigs with "Blues" carved into their steel bellies. A mural of blues singers marched together around the room, circling the crowded restaurant. Brandon ordered a Boulevard Single-Wide IPA and kept his aviators on, conjuring the spirit of Eric Church.

The band finished setting up and plugging in. We knew with the first chord that they would be fantastic. Brandon and I made eye contact and grinned, nodding to the music. He drummed on the table. He played air guitar.

"Isn't this great?" I asked the kids.

"This is so great!" I said again.

"Uh-huh," they murmured.

"When will our food be here?"

"I need to go to the bathroom."

After dinner I took a few photos of my boys with Brandon and then a selfie with Lydia, the little girl who is quickly becoming a young woman with her own dreams that are inextricably tangled with mine in ways she can't imagine.

"I just love live music," I said with a sigh.

And in their high, falsetto echo, they all said, "I love live music!"

Long Winter

Cowritten with Brandon Davis Wells

I've been chasing down the daylight
swinging hard to hit the highlights
but the way the darkness edges in
it makes me splinter
looks like it's gonna be a long winter

The kids have all grown used to
learning everything on YouTube
schoolwork's done and the family's
all here for dinner
looks like it's gonna be a long winter

CHORUS
We'll beat a path around this neighborhood
let the chill chisel our dark moods
your palm against my palm
I'd walk all night to keep this calm

I'll wake and meet the day before the dawn
maybe brew a pot and read who's gone
we got along the best we could
walked the dark before and we're still good

This year has been a constant battle
daily losses got me rattled
now the cold we're sinking in
it leaves me bitter
looks like it's gonna be a long winter

CHORUS
We'll beat a path around this neighborhood
let the chill chisel our dark moods
your palm against my palm
I'd walk all night to keep this calm

This year has been a constant battle
daily losses got me rattled
now the cold we're sinking in
it leaves me bitter
looks like it's gonna be a long winter

Chapter 12

Change of Plans

We live the given life and not the planned.

—Wendell Berry

Our final Wells Out West destination was unlike any of our other planned stops, which had revolved around the Great Outdoors. At St. Louis's City Museum, the kids crawled up and through the maze of metal and netting outside, explored each floor of wacky manufactured wonders, and played pinball for hours.

Recently Brandon said to me, "You know, that was probably the last time they were kids." The revelation stung a little, but he was right; if we returned to the City Museum again the next summer, it wouldn't have been the same. Everything would have already changed.

It all happened so quickly, this revolution, even though it felt so slow and eternal when it began. Our children were once just a glimmer of people we hoped for. By the time Henry is eighteen, their childhoods will have accounted for only twenty-three years of our lives. For how full it has been, it is still hard to believe that it will be over soon.

The Wells Out West trip rolled to its conclusion, skipping past the Gateway Arch and ending with a quick stop at a university outside of Columbus for a tour of the Next Phase of Our Lives.

I think I'm ready for it? As ready as I've been for any stage of my life? As if I have any notion of what the next stage holds, let us now pretend that the Plan will stand, all shall go exactly as we've predicted, and unlike the last forty years of my life, there will be absolutely no surprises. Right?

I started my new job on August 1, three days after we got home from our trip and two days after I turned forty. At eight each morning, I drove a quarter mile away from my home office to unlock the door to my campus office. After eight hours underneath the headache-inducing fluorescent lights, I invested in several floor lamps and never flicked the fluorescents on again. I organized files and relearned the bureaucratic workflow of faculty supplemental contracts. I met with each of my three bosses once a week, often via Zoom. The MFA summer residency ended and the fall semester began.

I came home completely depleted.

Several weeks into my new job, Brandon asked, "So, how was your day?" as we walked our loop with the dogs.

"Exhausting," I sighed, massaging the bridge of my nose. "Boring. Infuriating. Exhausting."

A woman has to know her limits, and I found mine.

"I'm going to give it three months," I said, not really believing myself even as I said it. "If I'm still grumpy and irritable and unable to keep writing while doing this job, I will quit and go back to freelancing."

"Do whatever you have to," he said. At that point, Brandon had already quit his job and was on the brink of beginning the fall semester, ready to finish the last year of his seminary degree. "We'll be okay. We'll make it work."

I was determined to stick to the Plan. What am I, some wimp, some chronically ill wimp? I'm a worker! I'm a *hard* worker! No heart? I'm *all* heart! So I rolled up my sleeves, grabbed onto my bootstraps, buckled up, hunkered down, and put my nose to the grindstone. I scheduled meetings across campus and made plans for grant writing and certificate programs, conferences and international travel. This was the job that I had been given, and this was the Plan. I would make it work, by God, even if it killed me.

Six weeks into my new job, I signed up for a meditation class at church led by my friend George. I thought it might be good for me to just sit in the Lord's presence for a little while each week. George invited us to read over a psalm and then do just that—sit in the Lord's presence. I settled in and closed my eyes. The half a dozen other folks around me did the same.

"Sarah," God said. I was just sitting there, minding my own business, trying to be open to hearing God's voice.

"Sarah," God said. He was sitting in one of our patio chairs on my deck in the shade of the towering oak trees, clasping both of my hands in his as if he was pleading with me. "I gave you all of these opportunities to do what I made you to do with joy and with freedom. And you chose stability and insurance."

I burst out in tears. Well, it was more like ugly sobs. If you've ever been scolded by God, maybe you can relate. This was not the Laughing Jesus. This was the Firm but Tender, Loving, and Direct Father. *Sarah*, he said. *I gave you all of these opportunities. You chose stability and insurance.* I immediately knew that if I didn't do something about my job, I'd be living in disobedience to whatever God has for me. That felt icky, devastating, and impossible.

Maybe you're like me. When someone says they heard from God, my first tendency is to roll my eyes. Sure, sure you did. Before, if someone told me they felt like God told them to quit a good job, I'd say, "Good for you!" while my face betrayed me. *Really? Don't you think that's irresponsible? Aren't you being a little presumptive? The Creator of the Universe took the time out of his day to speak to* you?

For so long now I've waffled on the idea of God's Plan, but I can't really do that now. *God* told *me* to choose joy and freedom. He *told* me. Yes, I heard the Creator of the Universe—who has given us everything that exists, breath and hope and dust bunnies and daylilies—tell me to live my life, my whole life, my everyday life, abundantly.

That was not my Plan.

Ten minutes later, when George drew us all from our meditations and back into the room, I couldn't stop blubbering. "I have to quit my job," I said through tears. "I think I have to quit my job." I wiped my nose and repetitively smeared the palms of my hands against my wet cheeks, trying to stop crying.

All I could think about was how humiliating it was going to be to resign from my job. I was going to disappoint so many people—Dan who basically custom-designed the job for me, Hilary and Maura who advocated for me, my three bosses, the alumni of the MFA program, the students in the honors program, the students in the MFA program, the president of the university, the new dean . . . and oh, no, what would my dad think? What about the kids? What about all of my friends in Ashland? I would look so foolish. They would think I was a failure. They would all be so disappointed in me. I thought of all of their faces while I sat blubbering through the rest of the meditation class.

Who just quits their job?!

Besides all that, I'd have to say goodbye to the kids' free tuition, farewell to our mediocre but adequate health insurance. I had dropped most of my freelance clients since August, too. Would I ever get that work again? How could God tell me to do this? Oh, and my husband was enrolled full-time at the seminary and currently unemployed while waiting for approval to substitute teach.

But *God* told *me* to *quit* my *job*.

"Do you want to take a walk?" my friend Colleen asked on the way out of church. I hesitated, unsure of whether I should unload all of my troubles on someone else's shoulders. But even then, I felt the Holy Spirit nudge, *Go. I have more I want to say to you.*

"Yes," I sniffled.

I texted Brandon, "I'm taking a short walk with Colleen before coming home."

It was a beautiful, clear September day in Ohio. Colleen and I walked the one-way street toward Freer Field. Our family lived on the street that bordered Freer Field throughout our children's younger years. We spent many afternoons frolicking through wildflowers, foraging for raspberries, and playing in the creek. We were lucky to have such a gorgeous span of nature right in our literal backyard when the kids were so small; we could sit on our brick patio and watch them run far into the distance, ever and always in sight but just out of listening range. Back then, I worked at the same university. Back then, Brandon was the one who was home with the kids, traveling on the weekends for work. Back then, I would never have dreamed of living in a town with sidewalks, until I did. I would never have dreamed of leaving the university, and then I did, and now I'm back again, apparently leaving again.

Not once has the life I dreamed for myself unfolded the way I imagined. It all just happened, wonderfully, tragically, chaotically, beautifully, some of it chosen, most of it surprising, all of it given.

Freer Field spills over into a wooded area filled with mature pines and oaks and maples. Colleen and I walked along the asphalt path that loops through the field to the forest, slowing and strolling as we navigated our way into the woods.

I told Colleen everything—how I felt like God had given us this job at the university, but maybe I had been wrong. Maybe I had misread the tea leaves.

"Well, obviously I have, because God just told me," I sniffled and laughed. We walked along the paved path, the leaves above us still bright green but with a hint of color on the cusp of breaking through.

The color of leaves in the fall is actually the color of leaves all year long—the green of chlorophyll just dominates during the growing season. You can see a tree's hidden colors in the spring, right as the buds burst through and before the chlorophyll starts collecting energy from the sun's rays. All spring and summer and into the fall, the cloak of green is necessary for growth, but when autumn comes and a tree draws down its resources for winter, that's when it shows its true colors. For the brief season, the tree is its most bold—dare I say joyful and free—version of itself: bright, radiant, and preparing for a long season of rest.

The trees didn't plan for it. The trees didn't earn any of it. The trees just accept the givenness of all things.

"Why don't we sit down and pray?" Colleen suggested. I was still sniffling and weeping, so I nodded and settled down next to her on a bench among the towering oaks and maples in the woods. Colleen sat quietly next to me, holding space for me and God to hang out for a while. I closed my eyes and breathed in, then out. "Lord, I surrender to you Dan's disappointment in me. I surrender Hilary's disappointment in me. I surrender . . ." I rattled off the names of everyone I would be disappointing, silently, in my head. The list seemed long. As I started to run out of names, I started to run out of tears. My breathing calmed. My shoulders relaxed. I took a deep breath and felt stillness, the weight of people's opinions of me lifted and replaced by a gentle and tender love. *This is my daughter, whom I love. In her, I am well pleased.*

I am not disappointed in her.

In her book *An Altar in the World: A Geography of Faith*, Barbara Brown Taylor writes about her search for God's Plan for her life. She says, "Then one night when my whole heart was open to hearing from God what I was supposed to do with my life, God said, 'Anything that pleases you.' 'What?' I said, resorting to words again. 'What kind of an answer is that?' 'Do anything that pleases you,' the voice in my head said again, 'and belong to me.'"

Do anything that pleases you.

I gave you all of these opportunities to do what I made you to do with joy and with freedom, and you chose stability and insurance.

In the days after Jesus rose from the dead, Peter went back to work. He had just spent three years walking alongside the Real Life Actual King of the Universe, but that was all over now. It was time for Peter to roll up his sleeves, grab onto his bootstraps, buckle up, hunker down, and put his nose to the grindstone.

"I'm going fishing," Peter said.

Later, after feeding him a breakfast of fish, Jesus asked Peter, "Do you love me more than these?" The footnotes say "more than these others do," as in, more than your brothers, more than your disciples, more than these other guys love me, but I think that Jesus is asking about the fish.

Do you love me more than these fish? Do you love me more than sustenance? Do you love me more than provision? Do you love me more than comfort? Do you love me more than a safe life? You are a good fisherman, Peter. You could make a good living with my miraculous hat trick of overflowing nets. But if you love me more than what these fish can give you, I have a different mission for you.

Jesus asked Peter three times if he loved Jesus, then followed each of Peter's answers with new instructions, "Feed my lambs . . . take care of my sheep . . . feed my sheep."

Like Peter, there was a way that seemed to be right for me, a fishing boat that was reliable and known, but in the end, going back into a role I had grown out of years ago felt like death.[17] And Jesus didn't come to crush, kill, and destroy but so that we may have life to the full.[18]

I once had a great life, working as an administrator for an MFA program. I once had a great life, working as a senior managing editor for a business school. I once had a great life, working as the content marketing director for a marketing agency. And then one day, a global pandemic happened, I got sick, and when I didn't get better, everything changed. In all of my suffering and weakness, God met me. God met me with mercy. God met me with grace. God met me with open arms. God greeted me with tenderness. God was never disappointed in me. God called me home. God said, *Do anything that pleases you, and belong to me.*

The day after my walk in the woods with Colleen, I put in my two weeks' notice without shame or embarrassment. If God invited you back into joy and freedom, would you be embarrassed? He *has* invited you into joy and freedom. So maybe don't wait anymore and just

---

17 Proverbs 14:12.
18 John 10:10.

accept that gift already. I couldn't wipe the smile off my face. I only felt kind of bad that I was so at peace with this decision.

Leaving my job and obeying Jesus felt like finding the pearl of great price, like finding the treasure in the field, like selling everything to buy that same field. I bought the field with joy and freedom at the price of stability and insurance. The field is wild and growing. There are wonders unknown just waiting to be discovered. I do not know what we will find in this field, but I know that it will be joyous. I know that it is held together by Christ. I know that it will be always and forever infused with love.

I devised a Plan to give my family moments to experience God in the wilderness, and we each found glimpses of God there through our individual lenses. Now we're back in our morning coffee and afternoon dog-walking routine, and here God is, in the texture of the fallen leaves, in the quiet of an empty house, in the anticipation of another month flipped over in the calendar, another moment held golden that is here and soon will be gone, replaced by yet another present for us to honor.

In the given life with all its growing pains and limitations and endings, there are limitless opportunities to experience awe if we remain curious, rooted and reaching in this wild pasture where Christ is the Shepherd, the Comforter, the Lord. Christ is with us in this given life, holding us and all things together, and that means we don't have to.

For so long I have worried and wondered whether and if there is a particular good and true and right Plan for your life and mine, scripted and orchestrated by a loving God. I looked to the sky and longed for that great expanse to clear and open so I could grab a glimpse of the vast beyond, as if those stars might hold all of the awe in the universe.

From my driveway in the summer, I can see the Big Dipper. In December, Orion's Belt shines between the trees. Here is the pearl. Here is the treasure. The evidence of God's steadfastness is right here, above and below, within and beyond. Life isn't planned. It's all given, wrapped in joy and adorned with freedom.

The gift is a far grander adventure than any I could have dreamed.

The Spill Over

I try to love the world but I can't
seem to make it past my own property line.
The landscape beds are long neglected, tan
stalks from last year's grass mingle, broken,
with spring's new growth. How will I ever
get to the starving children in Africa,
the refugees in Gaza, the millions weather-
affected in changing climates? Pick a

route and drive a mile, there's more to love
than I can grasp in my two hands, though I try
to make a space for dying things to rise
among my weeds, try my best to prove
that love can't be contained or framed in 4' by
10' beds. Come in, come over, eat dinner. I

struggle to love the world but I can feed you.

Epilogue

What I sensed God telling me about joy and freedom in October 2022 changed my life. There was no turning back; God had shown me the pearl of great price—that the treasure in the field is a life of obedience to the God of the universe, listening for the Voice and trusting Love to hold all things together. Could there be anything better than joining forces with Unconditional Love and following that Love wherever it may lead?

We sought to follow that lead as Brandon started job hunting during his final semester of seminary in the spring of 2023. I was gut-level certain that God wanted us to be in Ashland, that we had important work to do in Ashland, and that he would make a way for us to stay in Ashland. And he did. After sending many out-of-state applications, Brandon got a job working at Ashland University in the Center for Career and Life Calling as a career coach. It was a good job for him, but not the kind of job he could see himself doing forever.

Two years later, in June of 2025, several job opportunities in Ashland we thought for sure were for our family slammed shut so suddenly we didn't have time to pull our fingers out of the doorjamb. They were painful closures on pathways to a future we had hoped for, one that would cement our place in our small town. But it turned out those paths weren't ours to take.

After the second door closed, Brandon came home for lunch. He had texted me an hour earlier letting me know the job wasn't his. I couldn't keep it together; he found me weeping on the deck.

"It's okay," Brandon said. "We don't have to move."

"That isn't it," I mumbled through my tears. I just felt so brokenhearted over all of the hope deferred, all of the futures we had imagined for my husband and our family so recently dashed away. As I wept, something settled deep in my gut.

"I think we *should* move," I said. "I think we should seriously consider moving."

My word for 2025 was "abide." Rest and trust in the Vine, obey and follow and believe, drink deep the Living Water, abide in Jesus and only in Jesus. There have been many temptations this year to abide elsewhere—in new careers, in job titles, and most recently, in the safety of the known. As painful and difficult as it has been, I've tried to return to the One who calls me his beloved, trusting that no matter what, all shall be well, if only I abide with him.

All of the "nos" and "not yets" of the last two years brought us to a different question: "What would it look like if . . ." Can you imagine a future very different from this? What would happen if you opened the door to hope and possibility?

Brandon and I did a lot of dreaming and praying, talking and wondering. Our home, so recently depressed and heavy, reignited with a vibrant energy. As we considered "What would it look like if . . ." the space between us filled with joy and delight, surprise and hope, and an abiding peace that felt like the Lord saying, "This is the way."

One of my favorite "purpose and plan" verses in the Bible is not about the plan and purpose God has for our lives or how man makes his plan but the Lord directs his steps, it's this: "Whether you turn to the right or to the left, your ears will hear a voice behind you, saying, 'This is the way; walk in it.'"[19]

We could have stayed in Ashland. When we moved into our home on Berry Avenue, we called it our "death house." I had envisioned many Christmases there with grandchildren oozing from every hallway, our living room loud with lifelong friends and family. I loved the life we built for ourselves in Ashland and the people I got to serve in various capacities. I loved my book clubs and my deck and the woods

---

19 Isaiah 30:21.

and the birds and the deer that wandered through. I loved it all. We could have stayed. We could have made a way, and it would probably have been good.

But something deep called us away, and denying that feeling would have felt like disobedience.

In the wake of that one question, "What would happen if . . ." one by one, the threads that wove my heart to our community loosened. I felt it in my soul, an unraveling. It happened gently, as if I woke up from a deep sleep with a nasty knot in my hair. Instead of yanking and pulling, the Lord sat me down on a stool and stood behind me with a comb, working out each strand of what connected us to our town. He did so patiently, carefully, until all of a sudden I was free. All of those heartstrings loosened around my cherished community. All of those heartstrings loosened around my beloved house. All of those heartstrings loosened around my deck chairs and birds and trees, which I have never owned anyway but still called mine. All of those heartstrings loosened around my bedroom furniture, my flowerpots, my dish sets, and even my books (gasp!).

What if we just sold it all? What if we gave it away? Part of our purging of our worldly possessions was practical. We didn't want to spend thousands of dollars to move stuff we didn't *have* to move. But it also felt spiritual. It felt as if the Lord called us to go, sell our possessions, give to the poor, and follow him. In this letting go of things, I tasted what Richard J. Foster in his book *Freedom of Simplicity* called the "buoyant joy" of asking, "What can I do without?"

Part of me still can't believe this joy, this freedom. But somehow, someway, the Spirit has loosened every string and said, "It's okay. You can love the life you built here and do a new thing elsewhere."

"What is there for you to fear? Dear child of God, why do you not instantly cast yourself into the arms of Love? The only reason He extended those arms on the cross was so He might embrace you. Tell me, what possible risk do you take in

depending solely upon God? What risk do you run by abandoning yourself completely to Him?"

—Jeanne Guyon, *Experiencing the Depths of Jesus Christ*

In this season, our two oldest children are now legal adults and Henry is fourteen. Who knows where they will all end up? Henry is an adventurer, and also required by law to go with us. Because of God's mercy and grace, my mother is still cancer-free, and all of our parents are healthy. Grandchildren, if there will be any, are a few years into the future. As we considered our next steps, I asked Brandon, "What keeps us from going on an adventure? Where might we go? This is our window. If not now, then when?"

We talked about what it would look like to live in different cities. Our parameters included 1) someplace warmer, 2) someplace with a music scene, 3) someplace we knew at least one other couple, and 4) someplace we felt God calling us. That last one's harder to explain and involves intuition, an abiding sense of peace and joy, a gentle draw into the rushing waters. We decided to explore Wilmington, North Carolina.

We visited our friends in Wilmington. We leased a new house. We sold most of our things on Facebook Marketplace. We sold our Ashland house. We enrolled Henry in a new high school. And we moved. For the first time in my life, I live somewhere other than Ohio.

In this season, God invited us into a white water raft and said, "Strap in." It was as if we went back to the Narrows during the spring runoff, when all things are being made new, finally making our way beyond that bend in the canyon and striking out into the rapids of the Virgin River. The Guide said, "Pull in your oar, hang on, listen to Me, and you won't be tossed out. All shall be well. You're in for an exciting ride."

That seems to be the way the Lord works, moving in strange and unpredictable ways, going big when we expect little, staying small and quiet when we expect large and loud. I think maybe he delights in being a little wild and surprising. I mean, I delight in being a little surprising, so why wouldn't my God, who made me in his image? I bet he loves wild things.

I recently finished reading *Necessary Endings* by Dr. Henry Cloud, which helped me celebrate the reality that all things end. The only way for new things to begin is for some old thing to end. Endings are necessary for growth and movement, regeneration and change. It is the reality we buck against most of our lives. And that is okay, all of it is okay, the grief and the hope, the excitement and the tears, even the anger and the pain. That's what endings bring.

I serve a God who showed that every ending is also a new beginning, a God who died and resurrected, a God who is constantly doing new things and will continue to do new things.

I can't imagine a more wild and exciting way to live.

Acknowledgments

There aren't enough words to express how grateful I am to Brandon, Lydia, Elvis, and Henry for trusting me with parts of their stories and allowing me to share a glimpse into our lives with others. It is a responsibility and privilege I don't take lightly. I love the life we've built together. You are the best things.

Thank you to the editorial team at Root & Vine—particularly Conor, Stacey, and Kate—for asking me a simple question in 2020, "Do you know anyone who might like to write about creation care?" Our partnership gave me four years of meaningful work while I recovered from long-COVID and provided the initial skeleton for this book. And thank you to Miranda and Heather with Bracket for believing in me enough to trust me with this project. You two are incredible editors. This book is far better because of you.

My thanks also to our beautiful community in Ashland that held us together for so many years. Small Group Supper Club, Low E, Goldberry Girls, Park Street, 5 Stones, Mini-Mystic Book Club, Downtown Perk Ladies, Berry Avenue Book Club, Friday Night Field Stand Concessions Crew . . . y'all are what make Ashland "Someplace Special." We are blessed to have had such a beloved circle.

I'm grateful for the love and support of both my parents and Brandon's parents, through thick and thin, and the broader network of brothers, sisters-in-law, nieces, nephews, cousins, aunts, and uncles that may not be part of this particular story but have given our lives meaning, joy, laughter, and love far beyond the pages of any book. Thank you for loving us well.

And finally, thank you to Izzy and Ruby, you sweet and terrible fluffer nutters. For every thousand steps we've walked you've taken ten thousand with us, eagerly and faithfully. Thank you for your constant companionship through every paragraph of this book.

About the Author

Sarah M. Wells is the award-winning author of five nonfiction books and two poetry collections. Her work has been honored with four Pushcart Prize nominations and six Notable Essays listings in The Best American Essays. She is also the recipient of an Individual Excellence Award from the Ohio Arts Council. Sarah earned her BA in creating writing and her MFA in creative nonfiction from Ashland University. She writes regularly about nature and sustainability, contributes to a popular blog for women, and is poetry editor for *Relief: A Journal of Art and Faith*. Sarah and her family live in Wilmington, North Carolina.

Find her on
Facebook (smwells1982),
Instagram (@sarahmwells1982),
Substack (@palaceintime),
or online at sarahmariewells.com.

Also from Bracket Publishing

An honest, deeply relatable memoir about coming of age in
evangelical culture—and finding a way forward.

"A book to savor to the very last page."
—*Publishers Weekly* (starred review)

"A brilliant debut."
—Anne Bogel, host of the *What Should I Read Next?* podcast

Available wherever books are sold